Peace Knights
of the
Soul

Wisdom in 'Star Wars'

Jon Snodgrass, Ph.D.

INNERCIRCLE PUBLISHING

Peace Knights of the Soul
Copyright © 2005 Jon Snodgrass, Ph.D.

ISBN: 0-9755214-7-0

Cover Design by Jon Snodgrass
Created by Chad Lilly

All rights reserved. No part of this book may be reproduced in any form or by electronic or mechanical means, including information storage and retrieval systems, without permission in writing from the publisher, except by a reviewer who may quote a brief passage in a review.

Are You Aware?
www.innercirclepublishing.com

DEDICATED

TO GRACEN

CONTENTS

Dedication iii
Foreword by Jonathan Young ix
Introduction.. xi
Acknowledgements xii

1 ORIENTATION AND BASICS
    Principles 13
    Training 18
    Consciousness 21
    Identity 23

2 STORY AND HISTORY
    Magnitude Star Wars 29
    Impact of Star Wars 33
    Spirit of Star Wars 37
    Spirit of Star Trek 39

3 HOLY MOTION PICTURE?
    Parable of Faith 47
    Cosmic Hero 51
    Wisdom Hero 57
    Mystical Being 62

4 HISTORY AND MYTHOLOGY
    King Arthur 65
    Helen of Troy 70
    Holy Sophia 72

5 NOVICE AND MENTOR
    Mentor Seeking 79
    Lesson One: Willingness 84
    Beyond Willingness 87

6 APPRENTICE AND MENTOR
    Mentor Fighting 91
    Lesson Two: Patience 95
    Mentor Being 99

7 DISCIPLE AND MASTER
    Lesson Three: Phantom Enemy........ 103
    Retreat from Peace 110
    Lesson Four: Mind Power 112

FAITH AND PEACE

8
- Trapped and Defeated 119
- Resumption of Training 122
- The Evil Empire Ends 127

GENDER AND SEXUALITY

9
- Female Knights 135
- Naughty Knights 137
- Romantic Tales 141

ORIGIN AND TRANSMISSION

10
- Bunch of Sithies 149
- Chosen Child 153
- Elder Tribunal 156
- Conspiracy 160

TRAINING AND PRACTICE

11
- *Phantom Fiend:* Mariano E. Meléndez .. 167
- *SITH Lord:* Lucho Calvo-Guerrero 172
- *China Doll:* Mui Lam 175
- *Four Strangers* Paulo Dionisio 178
- *Far From Home:* Qiao (Jo) Kang 182

DRILL AND REVIEW

12
- Novice: Willingness 185
- Apprentice: Patience 188
- Disciple: Phantom Enemy 190
- Master: Mind Power 194

IDENTITY AND DESTINY

13
- Right of Passage 197
- Remembrance 200
- One Force 206

APPENDICES

- *Wisdom Test* 209
- *Canon of Star Wars* 211
- Bibliography 213
- Filmography 218
- Index 219
- Glossary 224
- Contributors 225

ILLUSTRATIONS

Four Basic Principles	17
Youth Meets Sage	19
Taken by the Weirds	28
Mythological Legacy	36
Unspectacular Heroes	41
Good and Bad Forces	49
Mythological Intention	50
Spiritual Computers?	54
Rational Faith	57
Twin Self	59
Ranks of Knights	66
Young King Arthur	67
Female Knights	73
Types of Crosses	75
Resistance	81
Willingness	85
Willingness Not	89
No Mas!	102
Chicanery	107
Helmet Headed	108
Reverse Perspective	115
Guiltless	131
Anticlimax	133
Allah and Shaitan	134
Bounty of Love	145
Precocious Robot	154
Knight and Slave	156
Pushed From Grace?	159
Ready to Enlist	166
Peace Poem	183
Peace Knight Path	196

THE HERO'S JOURNEY

Some books take the reader to a place beyond ordinary knowing. Such is the case with this exploration of the wisdom in *Star Wars*. By drawing on the world's wisdom traditions, Jon Snodgrass unlocks the spiritual secrets in the biggest film series ever. He shows artfully how the film adventure contains profound guidance for the inner journey to faith.

The mythological underpinnings of *Star Wars* have been widely recognized as part of its enormous appeal. This dimension concerns the meaning of human experience and offers insight to those wishing to have a richer inner life. The films and this book reveal that the wisdom of the ancients can be alluringly present in contemporary form.

Jon Snodgrass reads the episodes of *Star Wars* as mystery tales and draws on his understanding of spiritual teachings to uncover its wisdom. If we look at the films through a symbolic lens, the life lessons are abundant. Whether the story takes place in the real world, or a psychological dimension, the pattern is the same.

Tragedy sets the story in motion. We can relate the films to times in our own lives when we have felt overwhelmed by personal difficulties. This is the summons, the call to the quest. The suspense of the films involves the threat of domination by evil powers and the protagonists have little control over larger forces.

We identify with the heroic character who is a regular person in an initiatory adventure. The event that launches the quest might happen to any of us. It might be the death of a parent, a divorce, a terrible illness, or a financial disaster. When something devastating happens, we can give up on life or rise to the occasion.

The two *Star Wars* trilogies then are mirrors of our inner dramas. To succeed, the individual's actions must align with universal forces, a synchronization that eliminates feeling helpless and facilitates transformation. During this difficult process we find that we are capable of more than we ever thought.

When enmeshed in a larger purpose, you are yourself, truly for the first time. You discover capacities you never knew before. You go through the threshold of change and meet key allies in an adventure. It is the jumping off point beyond which there is no possibility of return.

The symbolic meaning of the tales profoundly connects *Star Wars* to transcendent principles. Adolph Bastian (1826-1905) argued that myths from all cultures are formed from the same "elementary ideas." This is the *mono myth* — the one great story that each culture repeats in every era. The pattern reflects the deepest concerns of people.

Joseph Campbell (1904-1987) called it *The Hero's Journey* — the great initiatory tale told all over the world. His classic, *The Hero with a Thousand Faces* provided the template for George Lucas to shape the *Star Wars* adventures. Campbell elaborated on the stages described originally in the work of Arnold van Gennep (1873-1957) who outlined the rites of passage.

Campbell was a gifted conduit for the great wisdom traditions. He did not invent the theories of initiation, but provided a compelling distillation of the ideas. The hero undertakes a dangerous journey during which he is forced to face his own dark side and align himself with a higher power in the universe.

Lucas maintains that *The Hero With a Thousand Faces* was the first book that focused what he was doing intuitively. "It was all right there and had been there for thousands of years." Lucas read other works by Campbell, including *The Flight of the Wild Gander* and *The Masks of God*. He also studied tapes of Campbell's lectures.

Campbell thought Lucas clearly presented the elements of initiation myth and metaphor. Campbell said, "I saw things from my books being rendered in modern terms. I admire what he's done immensely. He opened a vista, knew how to follow it and was totally fresh. It seems to me that he carried the thing through very well."

Noble Quest

The Jedi Knights are, first of all, seekers. They are also aristocrats—as knights, they are part of the nobility. Lucas seems to have taken this detail from medieval legends where the protagonists are often of noble birth. But, their aristocratic status is a psychological symbol.

Fascination with the nobility is a staple in science fiction. This does not mean that the audience longs to live under the rule of royalty or that Jedi Knights are genetically superior beings. The symbolism is deeper still. It is a yearning for the greater meanings of all these roles.

The tradition of highborn titles included devotion to great causes. These were lives with purpose and dedication to service. The psychological significance is that we long for our inner nobility. The character and purpose associated with such positions is missing in our endlessly practical age.

As a psychologist, I am drawn to the implications of the Force as a form of per-sonal guidance. The idea of the Force speaks to those who seek a link with the divine. This theme is also of interest for those whose inner journey is framed as maturation. These two perspectives share common ground.

Bill Moyers in 1999 referred in *Time Magazine* to my work: "The psychologist Jonathan Young says that whether we say, 'I'm trusting my inner voice,' or use more traditional language — 'I'm trusting the Holy Spirit,' as we do in the Christian tradition — somehow we're acknowledging that we're not alone in the universe."

Moyers then asks Lucas, "Is this what Ben Kenobi urges upon Luke Skywalker when he says, 'Trust your feelings' "? Lucas replied, "Ultimately the Force is the larger mystery of the universe. And to trust your feelings is your way into that."

Lucas' comment supports a natural collaboration between the inner journey and the yearning for connection to the transcendent. For psychoanalyst Carl G. Jung (1895-1961) the unconscious held our most radiant qualities. Receptivity to its treasures is a central task in what he called *individuation*.

Beyond any other factor, the idea of the Force makes the *Star Wars* films more than just well done science fiction. The Jedi Knights describe the Force as an energy field that sustains all living things. This mysterious element is the key to the transcendent magic of the stories.

The potential of opening up to the Force is available to every member of the *Star Wars* audience although one should be cautious in approaching such mys-teries. When we become attuned to insights beyond our immediate and practical concerns, the effect may take us in surprising directions.

Listening to voices from deep within can change everything. Quiet pursuits like poetry and meditation can lead to daring action once you find a calling. Teaching is not much of a life until you see the face of a student excited about learning something marvelous.

WISDOM REVIVAL

My own associations with George Lucas have all been very positive. I sense that his quiet style conceals the depth and intensity of a seeker. He has always been gracious to me — and encouraging of the efforts to continue Campbell's important work.

The *Star Wars* series spans generations. Many who first saw the film as teenagers, now bring their children to see the prequels. The devotion of *Star Wars* fans is amazing. They camp out before the release of each new film. In Australian, more than 70,000 people in a poll declared themselves to be believers of the Jedi faith.

The impact of *Star Wars* on popular culture around the globe is immense. Its success mirrors the fascination with all things mythic. There has been what some call a mythic revival in the last thirty years, traced mainly to the work of Campbell and his influence continues to rise.

When the intellectual history of this era is written, the impact of Campbell's legacy will be a major event in our collective evolution. For many, their first glimpse of ancient wisdom was the lore depicted in *Star Wars*. Lucas has contributed to the awareness of the treasures to be found on the initiatory journey.

Peace Knights of the Soul displays an impressive understanding of the spiritual depth of the *Star Wars* epics. Jon Snodgrass relies on mystical traditions to illustrate the wisdom in the most successful film series of all time. By revealing primary sources, this book also contributes to the scholarship of myth. For those fascinated with seeking the meaning of life, this work is an illumination.

Jonathan Young, Ph.D.
Santa Barbara, California

For centuries power existed in the forces of nature and science sought its control. The social sciences taught that personal identity is based on anatomy, and that the brain and mind are one. The meaning of life was reduced to neuro-chemical processes and humanity was divided into racial groups that disregarded its common spiritual essence.

War dominated world history. During the 20th Century, unprecedented multi-national violence expanded the scope of warfare to new levels and set the era apart from all history. Seventy million people were killed in World Wars I and II. At the beginning of the 21st Century, hostilities between stateless nations and nation states, threatened the use of nuclear weapons.

On all sides, the escalating aggression was driven by a deep fear to establish peace through spiritual awareness. Believing the great myth of science that humans are racial beings, war is born out of perceived alienation from God's love. Since science invented microscopes and telescopes to see beyond appearances, peaceful solutions are conceivable and feasible.

Peace Knights of the Soul is an analysis of science fiction film and the transcendent principles illuminated in the genre. This book was written for anyone wanting to learn about non-violent thinking. It relies on ideas in *A Course in Miracles* (1976) a work of spiritual psychology to the effect that world peace begins in the mind. In this view, social change does not require mass movements, political action or military intervention.

This work introduces the principles of personal peace consciousness and is dedicated to one grandchild. It was written to help the author find this state of mind even if the planet decides to blow itself up. Neo and Trinity in *The Matrix*, Prot in *K-PAX*, and Luke and Leia Skywalker in *Star Wars* are prototypes. First you want peace of mind, then you become a peace knight and "the world" moves toward the Light.

ACKNOWLEDGMENTS

Helen Arana
Victoria Bowker
Sarah Cypher
Paulo Dionisio
Qiao Kang
James Kelley
Mui Lam
Chad Lilly
Claudia Martínez
Mariano E. Meléndez
Corinne Muramatsu
Rosalie Ortega
Tom Satorhelyi
Ernesto Vásquez
Kenneth Wapnick
Jonathan Young

ONE

PRINCIPLES

People wonder about their purpose in life and long for fulfillment. The historical record is filled with answers from over the centuries that appear in mythology as models of the hero. By courage and great deeds an action hero saves society to preserve a traditional way of life. But a wisdom hero uses knowledge to introduce a new way of thinking so that civilization may evolve through *consciousness* instead of social action.

A wisdom hero understands an abstract principle about the nature of human existence that contradicts conventional thinking. To common sense, a separate reality of social and natural forces confronts the individual. But deeper reflection reveals an empirically confirmed truth: reality is created entirely with the mind. You see a hostile world when you are angry and a peaceful world when you love and both are purely mental projections.

*Perception
=
Projection*

Just as Newton discovered that gravity governs the motion of physical bodies and Einstein found that energy consists of the mass of an object times the speed of light squared, a wisdom hero learns that the perception of reality is a projection of a mental state (P=P). You see what you preconceive; no reality exists apart from the thinker. This power of the mind is universal, meaning it applies to everyone, i.e., *the hero with a thousand faces.*

*The
New
One*

Not as a reward for achievement, nor as a title of distinction, but as a model for others to follow, the wisdom hero is called "Philosopher King" in Platonic theory, "Enlightened One" in Buddhism, "Disciple of Christ" in the *New Testament* and "Advanced Teacher of God" in *A Course in Miracles* (ACIM 1976). The figure is portrayed occasionally in motion pictures: *Forrest Gump, Powder, Contact, Star Wars, The Matrix, K-PAX* and *Signs.* The character and story may change, but the *archetype* remains the same over time.

For example, *The Matrix* (Warner 1999) is a film about a small band of men and women in the future who discover that reality is an illusion generated by a sinister and pervasive computer system. They rely on science, martial arts and an elected leader who is a common-person. Guided by Morpheus (Laurence Fishburne) and inspired by an Oracle (Gloria Foster) the Matrix is unplugged by Neo (Keanu Reeves). *The New One* is able to break computer control by relying on a greater power in his mind.

CONSCIOUSNESS:
AWARENESS OF A COLLECTIVELY SHARED MENTAL STATE OF ONENESS.
ARCHETYPE:
BASIC MODEL, IDEAL TYPE, TEMPLATE.

In *K-PAX* (Universal 2001) Prot, i.e., *Proto Human* (Kevin Spacey) arrives on earth from a future millennium or another planet. On the Internet, strange world itself, Prot is discussed as an alien invader of a human host (i.e., the porter of Prot). His origin, however, is secondary to his role as peace representative. Unfortunately, he is taken into custody by police, diagnosed as delusional and institutionalized by a psychiatric team led by (Jeff Bridges).

Prot does not protest his confinement and mistreatment. He wears sunglasses all the time to shield his eyes from an intense Light that ordinary humans cannot see that sustains him during his journey. No one comprehends his claim to be a "Light being," but his kind advice on the ward heals many grateful inmates and improves even the psychiatrist's relations with his wife and children.

Humanity Denies Insanity

The doctor debates whether Prot is a space traveler or psychotic, but fears, as a scientist, that Prot's plan to return home on a light beam is suicidal. Using hypnosis, the doctor discovers that Prot is "Robert Porter," an identity erased by the violent murder of his entire family. The trauma and earthly past repudiate his claim to be an extraterrestrial. Prot then is regarded as an earthbound victim of events so horrible, like all humanity, wrenched from heaven, he denies his insanity.

Knowing he is a "being of Light," however, even while persecuted in mortal form, Prot departs through his mind anyway and leaves behind a catatonic body. As a shadow of his potential to exist in the Light, the physician continues treatment, trying to coax Prot back to life on the ward. After credits roll, however, he looks through a telescope and smiles, visualizing that identity arises from the mind not the body.

In *The Matrix*'s sequel, *The Matrix Reloaded* (Warner 2003) world takeover by the malevolent computers resumes. While Neo acquires extraordinary physical abilities symbolic of his new role as wisdom hero, the audience is amused by choreographed martial arts duels and spectacular vehicle chases and crashes. The Sentinel Army relentlessly drills underground to destroy the last refuge of humanity in the spiritual self (Zion). Countless replicas of the ultra-obsessive fighter, Agent Smith, thwart the band's hunt for insight to deconstruct the Matrix on the surface.

Mind Not Body

Ultra Obsessive Fighter

Despite horrible setbacks, for example, that the Oracle turns out to be a virtual fraud, Morpheus steadfastly upholds the prophecy that *Neo is the One* to liberate humanity by standing in the Portal of Light. But not believing from within, Neo remains unphased. The Oracle tells him, "You just have to make up your own damn mind, Neo." Military might is doomed and so this bleak middle story awaits resolution in the next episode.

In *The Matrix Revolutions* (Warner 2003) Neo still lacks conviction and therefore, is caught in limbo between the Matrix and Zion. A new Oracle sends him through the computer fields to negotiate peace with the machines. Meanwhile, a rogue Agent Smith infiltrates Zion to destroy it from within and to take over the entire planet. Massive military rebellion fails. But relying on blind faith in a higher power and with the assistance of Trinity, Neo stops Agent Smith and ends Matrix rule.

The double trilogies of *Star Wars* also focus on personal transformation. The theme of becoming a master Jedi Knight unites the visual imagery, special effects, digital editing and marvelous stereophonic sound. Luke Skywalker bears a celestial name, wields a cosmic force and becomes a great wisdom hero by the end of the chronicle of six feature films (Chapters 2 and 3). An audience of millions witnesses an astonishing fact: our hidden divinity is a birthright.

Birthright Divine Identity

Luke Skywalker learns to trust in "the Force" and demonstrates in the finale that violence is never necessary and vengeance never justified in human affairs. His pathway is available to anyone who wishes to learn about a sacred power in their mind — also known as "God." "Jedi Knights" thus model the attainment of peace consciousness via intuitive wisdom. This was neither the official *Star Wars* story nor the intention of the director.

The transition to higher consciousness, however, is the theme of *Peace Knights of the Soul*. Selected science fiction film is used to illustrate four fundamental principles about how to become an avant-garde (futuristic) thinker like Luke, Leia, Prot, Neo and Trinity. The process requires no super human talents, nor is it restricted to elite players who inherit or merit the status.

Violence Never Necessary & Vengeance Never Justified

The principles (and stages) in gaining higher consciousness are:

FOUR BASIC PRINCIPLES

1. Willingness — Novice
2. Patience — Apprentice
3. Phantom Enemy — Disciple
4. Mind Power — Master

Your potential awakens when you decide to unlock your mind from the vise of an identity based on anatomy. The achievement is possible for anyone willing to initiate the process. "All are called but few choose to listen" (ACIM). "You are the one," *Neo Anderson* is told repeatedly in *The Matrix*. Neo and One are *anagrams* for "the new one" who acquires consciousness in the 21st Century.

These principles are introduced here in Chapter 1. The story and history of *Star Wars* are reviewed in Chapter 2. Chapter 3 analyzes the theology of the film series and compares it to *Star Trek*. The origin of the principles in history and mythology is discussed in Chapter 4.

How to become a peace knight is the focus of Chapters 5-8. Chapter 9 deals with the issues of gender and sexuality among peace knights. Chapter 10 concerns the teaching of peace knighthood to children. In Chapter 11 five college students discuss the application of the principles in their daily lives. Chapter 12 reiterates the four basic principles and Chapter 13 concludes the study.

ANDERSON: SON OF MAN.
NEO ANDERSON: NEW ONE SON OF MAN.
ANAGRAM: WORD GAME REARRANGING LETTERS TO FIND HIDDEN MESSAGE.

Training

Justly Evolving & Developing Individual

This book evolved while teaching human development to diverse students in a metropolitan university where the author has been as a professor of sociology for more than thirty years. The project was inspired by the forty-five minute middle-segment of *The Empire Strikes Back*, when Luke Skywalker meets Master Jedi Knight Yoda for the first time.

The writing took place in 1997 and coincided with the twentieth anniversary release of *Star Wars: Special Edition*. Never a die-hard fan, I enjoyed the classic trilogy and twenty years later was inspired to show classes *When Luke Meets Yoda*. The parallels to our situation became obvious in discussions about human development. As the instructor, I played the role of Yoda, and was qualified by having both the ears and the years for the job.

Power in the Psyche

Each quarter I learned from teaching. However, like a reused stone tablet (palimpsest) only faint markings of the original essay appear in this text. Encouraged to recognize the power of their minds, students responded with the resistance Yoda faced with Luke: bewilderment, indifference, incredulity, hostility and ridicule. "In the *esoteric* history of *Star Wars*," I informed them, "JEDI is an *acronym* for 'Justly Evolving and Developing Individual.'"

ESOTERIC: KNOWN ONLY TO INSIDERS.
ACRONYM: WORD FORMED FROM THE INITIAL LETTERS OF A NAME.

While some students were lost because they did not know *esoteric* and *acronym*, this bit of comic trivia baffled almost everyone at first. By introducing humor, however, I was trying to put novices (beginners) in a playful mood and to open their minds to new ideas about the forces that govern their lives. Real power rests right within the psyche. I also have been told, "You use humor to prevent 'peace knights' from being an idea taken too seriously."

YOUTH MEETS SAGE

When Luke Skywalker meets Yoda to be trained as a Jedi Knight, he encounters a sage of wisdom. Yoda represents the old and wise part of every person who knows coercion and violence are not necessary in human affairs. Luke at first is frightened and threatens to blast Yoda away. This epitomizes everyone's initial reaction that peace consciousenss is dangerous. People choose to fight with mentors and others to keep the idea away.

At first, Luke is insolent. Yoda retaliates by rifling his equipment, making fun of his attitude and pestering him with pranks. Yoda asks a question that puzzles me: how do these kids grow so big eating junk food? Incidentally, "Yoda" is not "Joda," who is Yoda's younger brother working in *Ciudad de México*. *Amores Perros* (Altavista 2001) depicts the brutality in this center of humanity.

Able to Laugh?

In mythology, the "trickster" is an agent of social change and even God sometimes is portrayed as a practical joker who helps us realize the truth by laughing with us at our foolish mistakes. When this strategy works, what was so awful before, just seems funny. No one is harmed nor offended because the real Force is always with you. When your mind is reliable and flexible, you recognize the *fun* in *fun*damental and are able to laugh.

Asked to explain what Yoda is actually doing, trainees usually claim, "Yoda is testing Luke." They are less clear about the nature of the test. After some hesitation and discussion, however, it becomes evident. They believe Luke is pledging the *Fraternity of Jedi Knights* and that Yoda is performing a ritual hazing. Accustomed to adversarial encounters with authorities, students expect obedience as a test for promotion and graduation.

Humor Disarms Temper

Yet, Yoda is genuinely playful, a true confederate, a reliable mentor, a fond companion and really funny. To the weary and the wary, however, he appears to be deceptive. They suspect that "the power of your mind," really refers to "the power of my mind," a check to see if you respect the system I represent long enough to be certified to join the social mobility club. But an old truism states: you recognize a mentor when you are ready to learn.

Before beginning his journey to faith and truth, Luke is anxious, suspicious and serious because he is determined to become a powerful warrior using technological weapons in a militant confrontation with evil. At the same time, he is afraid his mission to save humanity from doom will fail. *Metaphorically* caught in the same dilemma, students fear failure but are reluctant to examine their basic assumptions about life.

Always Unconditionally Loved by God

I am told, for instance, "Yoda acts goofy," and, "You're just an eccentric professor." Knowing that fear makes you witless, however, Yoda and I both laugh quietly at these accusations. We know humor disarms temper when you smile and trust that you are allied with a higher power who is allied with you. The fifth "commandment" of peace knighthood is: thou shalt lighten up because you are always unconditionally loved by God.

The acronym "JEDI" is credible until some dedicated *Star Wars* buff repudiates it, or I confess that it was made up. Most students, chuckle with nervous disbelief. Notes may be taken for examinations but peace consciousness remains controversial. "When I first heard about becoming a Jedi Knight," a student explained, "I dismissed it as preposterous. I was not going to participate in any make-believe battle for the galaxy."

METAPHOR: ABSTRACT IDEA PUT IN STORY FORM.

My purpose is to teach and to learn mental self-reliance, or as a young surfer put it in slang, "To have peace consciousness for real."

To trust your own mind is an "old-fashioned" idea and the ancient key to wisdom. Shakespeare wrote, *To thine own self be true.* Socrates' motto was *Know Thyself*, inscribed in gold letters in Greek on the portico at the Temple of Apollo on the slopes of Mt. Parnassus in Delphi and in Latin on a plaque over the doorway of the Oracle's kitchen in *The Matrix*.

Gnothi Sauton (Greek)
Temet Nosce (Latin)

CONSCIOUSNESS

Millions of people watched *Star Wars* but few saw its instructive potential because the gap between audience and hero is too wide. An ordinary lad becomes a great man but trapped within the insane maze of projected mind power known also as "society," viewers do not imagine a connection to the wisdom hero nor visualize their own potential. The solution to life's problems is thought to lie in outer forces beyond their control — a reaction that impedes personal growth.

God aka The Force

Figuratively, everyone pilots a starship and battles wicked demons in life. Like an idealistic adolescent, everyone wants excitement and validation during their journey to destiny. But defeating the commander of death and becoming the people's great hero is considered "a wild daydream." Then *Star Wars* remains science fiction fantasy about outer space rather than an inspirational film about earthly human potential.

Insane Maze of Mind Power Projected

Peace Knights of the Soul constructs a bridge to development called "peace knighthood." This is done first by analyzing Luke's story and then by identifying the exact procedure he follows to acquire higher consciousness. The reader then understands the process that is imbedded in the *Star Wars* context. In the finale, Luke says to Darth Vader, "I will not fight you, Father." This line alludes to having faith in God, also known as "the Force."

His decision is based on two basic principles (*Willingness* and *Patience*) and two advanced principles (*Phantom Enemy* and *Mind Power*) about how to proceed on the path of the wisdom hero. Most people are not motivated, however, because they believe power exists in the universe and not within their mind. Few realize that a method exists to gain freedom through introspective wisdom, rather than social action.

No Social Action

Just as you can workout to gain muscular strength, you can exercise to grow psychologically. *Star Wars* conveys this unique idea by relating it to a familiar story. These principles, however, are not stated explicitly by the green sage of the saga, Master Yoda, who teaches through demonstration but without verbal elaboration. As a mentor, he also offers insight to support and expedite the process.

Wisdom Not Action Hero

Never transmitted formally in schools and books, spiritual wisdom was taught orally between teacher to pupil in ancient times. Beginners traveled to a lodge, petitioned for admission into a secret order, and learned precepts and practices interpersonally from an adept (expert). "Hermetic" means "sealed off" and comes to us from the secret writings of the followers of *Hermes Trismegistus* (1st-3rd Centuries A.D.).

Peace Knights of the Soul openly walks the reader through the process of learning peace and associates each stage with the story as first taught to Luke by Yoda. The principle then is stated clearly, explained fully and related to contemporary times. These lessons in personal liberation lead step by step from Novice, to Apprentice, to Disciple, to Master, so that human development remains no longer a secret science for the specially endowed.

HERMES TRISMEGISTUS: "THREE TIMES GREAT" ANCIENT LEGENDARY TEACHER IN EGYPT SAID TO BE AN EARLIER INCARNATION OF JESUS.

Luke's achievement is prototypical for spiritual growth without the need for clergy, bible, sacrament, ritual or church. He learns that no evil, no sin and no devil can exist due to the presence of God, the "meta-mind," within the human mind. There is nothing that you can do, no matter how heinous, that changes God's love for you. "Only the dead have seen the end of war" wrote Plato, but with consciousness, even the living can have peace.

A peaceful person tries not to use physical force to resolve any dispute, including whether or not to undertake the journey to faith. Though you make a decision, you do not instantly illuminate, due to self-doubt (though theoretically it is possible). The sole purpose in acquiring peace consciousness is freedom from the illusion of all limitation in life. Under any kind of duress, however, you lose the awareness of God in your mind.

No
Evil
Sin
Devil

"Evil" stems entirely from ignorance about our origin in the Light, in the same way that darkness arises solely from the absence of the sun. No angry deity differentiates between good and bad people to mete out eternal damnation in an afterlife. A wisdom knight endeavors to maintain awareness of eternal love through insight during an earth-bound transit. Be Willing and be Patient, therefore, to see the Phantom Enemy and to discover Mind Power that ends the strife in your life.

WPPEMP

Identity

The Force in *Star Wars* is depicted as the possession of a special power by certain individuals and members of their family. In *Phantom Menace*, "midi-chlorians" are microscopic organisms in the cells of human tissue that genetically transmit the Force from one generation to the next. As a hereditary condition, the quantity of these microbes establishes eligibility for training elite Jedi Knights.

No
Angry
Diety

In the *Making of Episode I*, George Lucas says, "The midi-chlorians have brought Anakin into being as 'the chosen one' who will balance the universe." Liam Neeson, an actor, reported that Lucas explained to the cast during filming that there are "thousands of bacteria in our system" and that "some people had a stronger strain of these bacteria than others did." (Bouzereau 1999). In this context, "bacteria" apparently is another name for "midi-chlorians." Neeson added that he found the idea "fascinating" and "believable."

Sith =

The *Star Wars Encyclopedia* refers also to "Dark Side evil" that "courses through the veins" of some non-Jedi Knights. "The group from whom evil descends" is known as "the Sith" and Darth Vader is the "Lord of the Sith." Based on some fantastic bodily attribute, genetic inheritance accounts for the presence of the Force among select groups in the galaxy. But Sith is an anagram for excrement.

Controversial among fans, midi-chlorians received little debate in the media. Kevin Blades, creator of a now disbanded website *(Star Warz Legacy)* argued that midi-chlorians "despiritualized" the Force by putting a *gnome* in the *genome*. In *The Myth of the American Superhero* (2002) John Lawrence and Robert Jewett claimed that midi-chlorians resemble World War II Nazi slogans like, "We think with our blood." Their chapter is entitled, "Fascist Faith in the *Star Wars* Universe."

Lawrence and Jewett assert that the superhero in *Star Wars* relies on *redemptive violence*, but this idea overlooks the ending of the sequel trilogy. It is exactly the reverse — Luke throws his weapon away and stops fighting (Chapter 8). Stating that *Stars Wars* ". . . offered a rationale for Timothy McVeigh's indiscriminate killing in Oklahoma City," the authors are extremists too. Yet, their work won the Popular-American Culture Association Book of the Year Award in 2003.

GNOME: AGELESS ELF IN FOLKLORE.
GENOME: UNIT OF GENETIC INHERITANCE.
REDEMPTIVE VIOLENCE: SAVED BY USING VIOLENT MEANS.

In *The Empire Strikes Back*, the fifth installment, Yoda tells Luke, "A Jedi's strength flows from the Force" (not the bloodstream). Referring ambiguously to social or biological transmission, Yoda also says to Luke, "The Force runs strong in your family." But *Star War's* book of genesis, *Phantom Menace,* is regressive. "The Force" appears more biological than mystical in the prequel than in the sequel — more explicitly racial in the second trilogy.

"I need a midi-chlorian count," Qui-Gon Jinn announces in *Phantom Menace,* but true peace knights count on consciousness. That the hero in *Star Wars* is stereotypically white, blond and male, or that Darth Vader is the black-clad, blue-eyed devil, are irrelevant to serenity, which is accessible regardless of age, gender, body type, sexual orientation, residence, nationality or environmental condition. Homo "sapiens" are "wise," so an anatomically based identity is simply mistaken.

Wise Homo Sapiens

Peace consciousness has nothing to do with parents, birth, ethnicity, blood type, body fat, or the hereditary molecule (cellular deoxyribonucleic acid — DNA). Identity is psychic, estab-lished by conceptual conditions not congenital ones. Wisdom heroes are not the genetically superior mutants of age-old fables. According to Jonathan Young in the *Foreword,* Jedi Knights are elite in that few meet the challenge to mature. Charges of racism and sexism, however, have plagued *Star Wars.*

Peace Not Race Consciousness

A New Hope, for example, was criticized for having few women and no dark-skinned actors. The voice of James Earl Jones was adopted for Darth Vader, but the actor was white. Jones accepted $10,000 for his voice-over work, but influenced by rumors that the film was destined to flop, he protected his career by declining screen credit (Baxter 1999). Ironically, the public now permanently associates his voice with the evildoer. Billy Dee Williams played a Judas-like character in *The Empire Strikes Back.*

Conceptual Not Congenital

Proposing to the ruling assembly to give absolute power to the future tyrant of the galaxy, Jar Jar Binks is set up to be scapegoated in the final episode, *Revenge of the Sith.* The accent and mannerisms of this computer-generated, goofy-eared amphibian in *Phantom Menace* stirred controversy (Eric Harrison, "A Galaxy Far, Far Off Racial Mark?" *Los Angeles Times*, May 26, 1999). Lucas said no ethnic stereotype underpinned the character and called the idea "absurd." Yet, an underground re-editing from stock tape, known as *Episode 1.1: Phantom Edit*, appeared on anti-Jar Jar websites in 2001 and cut the figure out of the film entirely.

Suffering Individual Through Hatred

Peace knighthood is self-initiated when you acknowledge a higher power in your mind. There is no other way — no mystical rites, training sites, geographical relocations, technical skills, support teams or special weapons that make it happen. You need not dodge bullets, walk on walls and ceilings, or be a flying martial artist. As illusions, like fighting windmills and puff dragons, biological prerequisites, supernatural talents and social action are irrelevant.

Everyone belongs to this "new breed" because it is entirely a club of the mind. In acknowledging your sacred right, you begin a psychological ascent. SITH is understood in this text, therefore, as an acronym for "Suffering Individual Through Hatred," a learned way of thinking. The absence of this awareness is the "original sin," in the fall of Anakin Skywalker depicted as the theme of the entire prequel trilogy (chapter 10).

Ego vs God

Imbedded in *Star Wars* also is the radical idea that suffering, especially that of the wicked Darth Vader, is a product of thinking. Once Luke sees that the war starts as a divided state of mind carried out between beings and planets, he realizes that what he thinks to be true about good and evil, defines his father and the whole universe. Thinking thus causes one or the other to prevail as "reality."

This message is not deliberately concealed, but unrecognized, in the same way moral lessons in parables remain obscure until clarified by the wisdom of a teacher. Superficially, the saga is about fight ing and war heroism, but more profoundly, it is about becoming a peace champion by not fighting. This choice is hard at first, because as veterans and refugees, due to our original decision to fight God, we perceive a war "out there" in the world.

Sage in the Psyche

A deeper understanding requires you to dispatch yourself to a remote location where it is safe to detach from "reality." You open to a sage buried deep in the bog of your own psyche. When you retreat and relax, sanity and serenity restore quickly. But woe unto the ones who harbor grudges about childhood abuses, for anger and fear are learned from the adults who acquired it from their parents and it is visited upon future generations (Chapter 10).

People do not think star peace is an alternative to star wars through a commission in consciousness. It seems impossible to believe that all conflict is designed, executed, contained, halted and eliminated within the mind. The knowledge that pain has no origin outside the ego, that in fact no malicious conspiracy exists, enables you to end all perceived inner and outer strife. To recognize that "the matrix" is an illusion does not require you to swallow a red, white or blue pill.

Waging war is the insane solution that has never worked historically. The famous Swiss psychoanalyst, Carl G. Jung, once said, "When you lose your temper, the battle is already lost," and Jung lost many. When you enter the wrong state of mind and forget your original reason for the trip to faith, the opposition looks formidable. When you regain your right mind, however, the conflict is resolved and adversaries dissolve.

Living in 'Reality'

To appreciate the principle of mind power is the hardest lesson for peace knights to learn, and it requires time, education and dedication. Knights of the third and fourth realms, apprentice and master, are rare but never extinct. A spiritual path is not an easy route

TAKEN BY THE WEIRDS

Date: Sun, 13 Jun 1999
From: neo@yahoo.com
Subject: "On Becoming a Jedi Knight"
To: jsnodgr@calstatela.edu

I came across your article, "On Becoming a Jedi Knight" and was taken by the wierds. I was searching for information or a "teacher" in the ways of mind and spirit using the term "Jedi" as a pathway to the knowledge I seek.

Your article is like none other I have seen. Do you really believe the way your speak? Are you truly one of the mind? I am a 19-year-old high school graduate who seeks to learn the ways of wisdom and I see possibility in your words. Please respond. Thank you.

———

to follow, but not as hard as living in "reality" and never getting started. Consigned to a body in time and space, the riddle of identity and destiny is solved with wisdom.

Two

STORY & HISTORY

MAGNITUDE

In chronological order, the six acts of the *Star Wars* drama are:

Episode IV: *A New Hope* (1977)
Episode V: *The Empire Strikes Back* (1980)
Episode VI: *Return of the Jedi* (1983)
Episode I: *Phantom Menace* (1999)
Episode II: *Attack of the Clones* (2002)
Episode III: *The Revenge of the Sith* (2005)

A New Hope, written and directed by George Lucas, remained the highest-grossing domestic film for more than twenty years until the debut of the *Titanic* (Paramount) in 1997. Lucas also produced the sequels, *The Empire Strikes Back* and *Return of the Jedi*, but chose Irvin Kershner to direct the former and Richard Marquand to direct the latter. (Kershner was one of George Lucas's professors at the University of Southern California School of Cinema and Television in the 1960s).

A New Hope is listed as fifteenth on the American Film Institute's roster of 100 greatest American films. But a public opinion poll conducted by AFI ranked *A New Hope* first, *The Empire Strikes Back* second and *Return of the Jedi* sixth. These three films comprise the first *Star Wars* trilogy — the most popular series of motion pictures of all time.

As of 2004, five out of six *Star Wars* films, were the most lucrative franchise in terms of domestic box office receipts ($1802 million). The closest rival was the series of twenty James Bond films ($1217 million). The ten films of *Star Trek* ranked fifth ($758 million) and *The Matrix* trilogy placed eighth ($592 million) (boxofficereport.com).

Back in 1978, Twentieth Century Fox Studios told theater owners, "If they wanted to show *The Other Side of Midnight*, they would also have to book this science fiction film, *Star Wars*," wrote film critic Mark R. Leeper. Today, no one remembers the old melodrama about the romantic life of shipping magnate Aristotle Onassis. Only thirty-two theaters scheduled the release of *Star Wars* and no one predicted its phenomenal future.

Fox accountants estimated a total return of $35 million for *A New Hope*, but the actual figure is $784 million worldwide gross. The film's success is the result of the combination of: an old-fashioned adventure story, revolutionary special effects, a John Williams Oscar-winning musical score in ultra stereophonic sound and the unusual humor of two sentient robots with obstinate personalities just like real human beings.

"*Star Wars* was obviously a ground-breaking film from the first moments of the film," continued Leeper. "Just showing a field of stars, *Star Wars* did something that no other film had ever done. It panned the camera upward . . . space scenes had always been done [before] with a fixed camera." Thus, this motion picture had panoramic vision from the outset. But it was originally written in pencil in a notebook by a shy young man from Modesto (modest) California.

Prequel
Sequel
Postquel?

For the twentieth anniversary in 1997, Lucas theatrically re-released the *Star Wars Trilogy Special Edition*, "digitally remastered" as videos in 1994, to coincide with the distribution of a new set of toys. Four and one-half minutes of visuals were added, the sound track was enhanced and special effects modified, i.e., matte lines erased and a gruesome ice monster appeared.

At the same time, plans were announced to produce three new episodes, called "prequels" because they precede the trilogy in time. "Prequel" was a new word, the opposite of sequel. The prequels focus on the rise and fall of Anakin Skywalker, who becomes the notorious Darth Vader. Like long flashbacks, the future is explained by events in the past. *Attack of the Clones* was the sequel to the prequel that came after the first trilogy.

The prequel titles were closely guarded secrets, known to the public only as: *Star Wars: Episode I* (1999) *II* (2002) *and III* (2005). Media leaks about *Episode I*, however, sent fans into frenzy and it was rumored to be called *Balance of the Force*. Someone on the Internet, who had no ties to Lucasfilm, apparently made up this title. ["Star Wars II" and "Son of Star Wars" are names for a missile air defense system launched by former President Ronald Reagan (1911-2004)].

The trailer for *Phantom Menace* announced its title and marked Lucas's return to directing for the first time since *A New Hope*. *Phantom Menace* opened Memorial Day 1999 and was designed to sink the *Titanic* in terms of box office receipts and popular appeal. The *Titanic* filmmakers were supposed to put out a distressed "Mayday" and go down on the charts.

The *Los Angeles Times* (May 10, 1999) quoted Lucas saying he would be disappointed if *Phantom Menace* did not become "one of the top 10 grossers of all time." In 2003, worldwide sales of theater seats were estimated to be: *Titanic* $1,835.4 million versus *Phantom Menace* $925.6 million (boxofficereport.com). The budgets for the two films were $115 to $200 million. *Titanic* still holds the revenue record for a single release, but *Star Wars* is the highest grossing franchise ($1792 million).

Attack of the Clones was matched against *Spider-Man* (Columbia Pictures) and earned respectively: $86.1 million to a record $114.8 million in three days in 2002. The contest was flawed because the former opened on a Thursday at 1500 fewer theaters. However, it held the midweek one-day record of $30.1 million. *Spider-Man* opened on a weekend and earned $43.6 million. *The Matrix: Reloaded* overtook *Attack of the Clones* on worldwide box office charts as of October 2003 ($735 to $648 million).

Spoilers: About final *Episode III*, Lucas has announced, "It's a tragedy." It is a darker story for smaller audiences because the bad guys win. Film Threat, a Hollywood website devoted to independent filmmaking (filmthreat.com) had predicted correctly for years that *Episode III* would be titled *Revenge of the Sith*. An update to their synopsis might read as follows:

SPOILER: INFORMATION DIVULGED BY VIEWERS OR REVIEWERS REVEALING THE PLOT OR ENDING OF A FILM.

> *Anakin is expelled from the Order of Jedi Knights and descends to the Dark Side as Darth Vader. Padmé gives birth to Luke and Leia, and is assassinated. Obi-Wan becomes a general in the Clone Wars and Chancellor Palpatine ascends to power as the evil emperor. The republic passes and the evil empire arises. The Jedi Knight Council disbands, Jedi Knights are exterminated and Yoda retreats to regain his sanity.*

The popularity of the series made Lucas a celebrity and the thirty-fourth richest man in the world. A *New Hope* was nominated for ten, and actually won five academy awards, including one for editing by Lucas's wife Marcia. But Lucas himself has never received an Oscar. The wicked Darth Vader was featured on the coveted cover of *Time Magazine* (May 1980) and the triad of martyrs, Qui-Gon Jinn, Obi-Wan Kenobi and Anakin Skywalker on the cover for the premier of *Phantom Menace* in April 1999.

Originally, there were also three proposed "postquels": *Episodes VII, VIII* and *IX*. *Star Wars* was envisioned as a "trilogy of trilogies," explained James Ward, Internet author of a satire on a hypothetical *Episode VII*. In interviews, Lucas has said that *Episodes VII-IX* will never be written because he has no story. Also, he will not allow any successor to carry on the series. He claims the prequel trilogy (*Episodes I-III*) will make clear why *Return of the Jedi: Episode VI* is the conclusion.

IMPACT

The Empire Strikes Back, the middle installment of the first trilogy, features the sudden appearance of a higher caliber of evil in the galaxy, Emperor Palpatine, who outranks Darth Vader as a fiend. Some reviewers objected to making the original villain a second because his vision of the "dark side" pales in comparison to his superior's. Profound guidance also shows up in this episode as the patron saint of Jedi Knights, Master Yoda.

The escalation of good and evil is based on Lucas's experience working with 20th Century Fox Studios. According to insider accounts, throughout the filming of *A New Hope*, there were intense struggles with stars, crew and studio executives. Hospitalized for hypertension and exhaustion, Lucas said at the time, "It's like fighting a fifteen-round heavyweight bout with a new opponent every day."

"Hollywood is the Death Star and Lucas is the eternal rebel," wrote biographer Dale Pollock (1990). Lucas quit as a director, withdrew from Hollywood and founded an independent film production company, Lucasfilm Limited, in Marin County, California, about an hour north of San Francisco. He found more evil in real life than conceived originally in the script.

An Anti-War Film

During the 1980s, President Ronald Reagan's Cold War Strategic Defense Initiative (SDI) was dubbed "Star Wars" by the media. Developments in laser technology made feasible a national ballistic missile defense shield. The proposed system coincided with the futuristic special effects of *Star Wars*, playing then in theaters and blurred the distinction between fantasy and reality. By 2004, the federal government had spent $130 billion researching the project.

Jean Renoir's 1937 classic French anti-World War I film was entitled *The Grand Illusion*. The son of the famous impressionist painter, Auguste Renoir, Jean Renoir had been a fighter pilot in "The Great War," as it was known. Within the context of World War II, the Korean War, the Vietnam War and the Cold War — wars that spanned Lucas' lifetime — *Star Wars* was an epic antiwar film series.

New Type Hero

Violence, genocide and threats of nuclear annihilation characterized the 20th Century. But suddenly — an unimposing figure appears — one who draws on inner resources for self and universal transformation. Lucas constructed a new type of hero to replace the wild, old-style gunslinger of his childhood, epitomized perhaps by the actor Ronald Reagan.

Without transforming into Superman and more innocuous than the mild-mannered Clark Kent, Luke Skywalker is able to "defeat" the bad guys just by being himself. Without violence and vengeance, an unprecedented non-violent climax to an action film, a modest young man vindicates the law of faith in a higher power.

Luke's journey is depicted from the time of his father's childhood (*Episode I*) to his father's courtship and marriage (*Episode II*) to his father's fall from grace (*Episode III*) to his own recruitment to the cause (*Episode IV*) to his struggle with destiny (*Episode V*) to his victory over evil (*Episode VI*) as the bearer of a mystical Force that ends universal warfare and liberates humanity forever from the tyranny of evil. This is accomplished solely by changing his mind, not by any social, political or military action.

Ends Violence & Vengeance

After World War II, the image of the hero was revised also in the films of Japanese director Akira Kurasawa, son of a samurai army officer. In *The Seven Samurai* (1954) "Ronin" are depicted as uprooted, masterless warriors in Japan in the 1600s, akin to roving western cowboys in the United States in the 1800s. They have lost their cultural identity and ties to social class, due to widespread social disintegration and moral corruption, but as individuals, they uphold the traditional ethical code of the samurai *(bushido)*.

The Seven Samurai was the first foreign film in the United States to be nominated for an Oscar for best picture. The term "Jedi" may have originated in Kurasawa's "Jidai Geki" films, referring to a "period drama" set in medieval Japan during the height of the samurai, as opposed to "Gendai Geki," which take place in contemporary settings. Internet reports claimed Lucas "mentioned in an interview that he saw a 'Jidai Geki' television program in Japan a year or so before the movie was made (*Episode IV*) and liked the word."

New Hero After WWII

In ancient times the hero was precisely the one who mediated between the strife-torn world of human affairs and the sacred realm of the divine. Divided and at war since the dawn of history, armies

MYTHOLOGICAL LEGACY

The story of Star Wars . . . has had such an influence on our culture that it prompted Joseph Campbell, one of the most original and influential thinkers of our time, to hail the trilogy as a masterpiece of "creative mythology" — a work of art that gives new depth and dimension to our sense of self and place in the universe. For millions of viewers, the Star Wars epic presents a special vision that incorporates the wisdom and symbols of age-old myths in dynamic new ways that speak uniquely and unforgettably to our modern day quest for meaning.

Mary Henderson, *The Magic of Myth*

---

have always claimed, in their legends, that God intervenes on behalf of their victory. In a secular version, knights were a class of soldier that arose in the Middle Ages to settle disputes among nobles.

Blending Reality & Fantasy

"I'm telling an old myth in a new way," Lucas explained in a *Time Magazine* interview with Bill Moyers in April 1999. Jedi Knights are thus representatives of the Force who help humanity reconcile discord. Their hallmark salutation, "May the Force be with you," is appeal to heaven for guidance in remediating earthly disputes. Lucas once said, "I don't see *Star Wars* as profoundly religious." Yet, an implicit spirituality may be another reason for its global impact.

Blending reality and fantasy, over 200 items from the Lucasfilm archives went on display in 1997 at the National Air and Space Museum at the Smithsonian Institution in Washington D.C. Emphasizing military costumes and weaponry, the exhibit was free to the public and credited by the *Washington Post* with helping the capitol city record a banner year for tourism. The exhibition toured nationally in 2000 and can be visited online (nasm.si.edu).

The curator, Mary Henderson, authored an illustrated, full-color, companion volume: *Star Wars: The Magic of Myth* (1997). Just as ancient stories entwine history and mythology, the exhibit and the book mythologize *Star Wars* culture. Joining Lindberg's *Spirit of St. Louis*, the Wright Brothers' *Flyer* and NASA's Space Shuttle *Enterprise*, *Stars Wars* was enshrined in national aerospace history.

Mystical Knightly Order

Terms from *Star Wars* were among 3,500 new words to enter the fifth edition of the *Shorter Oxford English Dictionary* in 2002. "Jedi," "the Force" and "Dark Side" were added along with "Klingon," "warp drive" and "mind meld" from *Star Trek*. "Jedi" is defined as an "invented name" for a "mystical knightly order." The themes of *Star Wars* and *Star Trek*, are contrasted in the next two sections.

Spirit of *Star Wars*

'The [religious] laws are in yourself,' Lucas is fond of saying," wrote biographer Dale Pollock (1990). The spiritual doctrine of the Force is explicit at times and left quite implicit at others. Either way, however, *Star Wars* addresses four metaphysical questions about life: who are we, where is our origin, what do we do with our lives and what happens to us after death?

Four Basic Life Questions

Overtly, the film series is known for its special effects and great adventure story. It is modeled on the old-fashioned, black and white serials of good versus bad in children's matinees shown in movie theaters in the days before television. But *Star Wars* actually offered Saturday evening entertainment for the whole family and suggested a righteous way to lead life.

On the one hand, *Star Wars* is standard dramatic fare: villainy and treachery, corruption and deception, romance and mystery — and an old-time action hero who triumphs in the end. It is preoccupied with technology, equipment, weapons, rank, spacecraft, crea-

META-PHYSICS: META = "ABOVE" PHYSICS, OR STUDY OF ABSTRACT PRINCIPLES GOVERNING LIFE.

Faith in the Force

tures, robots and planets. *Star Wars* proliferated and capitalized on action figures, guides to weapons, etc. A few reviewers condemned it as adolescent fantasy — boys playing combat in the shadows of World War II.

At times, *Star Wars* epitomizes a male action film genre. While not gratuitously violent, or even graphically bloody, exploration is secondary to aggression and not restricted to "Dark Side" players. To avoid captivity, for example, Princess Leia melts the face and skull of an imperial storm trooper with her laser pistol in the opening pages of the novel. In *Return of the Jedi*, she single-handedly strangles a crime lord to death using the chain that enslaved her.

Some people thought *Star Wars* wildly thrilling entertainment and remember how they enjoyed sitting around with friends talking cryptically like Yoda. Others despised it as a device for stringing together special effects. A model maker on the classic trilogy, Joe Johnston, is quoted as saying that the crew was never sure whether the story was a vehicle for special effects or special effects a vehicle for the story (Jenkins 1997).

Well known film critic Pauline Kael (1919-2001) called *Return of the Jedi* ". . . A flabby excuse for a lot of dumb tricks and noise." In retrospect, however, another point of view emerges concerning the saga's mythical foundation, profound theological premise, deep psychological meaning and humanistic promise. In the conclusion to the double trilogy, a universal law concerning spiritual transcendence is upheld by faith in the Force.

A glut of technical literature exists about *Star Wars* — paeans to locations, costumes, sets and hairstyles, but little has been written critically or analytically. In contrast, over the years, a variety of books have appeared about its rival, *Star Trek*. Paramount Studios introduced four new television series, an animated television series and ten *Star Trek* movies as of 2002, while the book franchise business thrived in the marketplace.

For twenty years, however, there were no television series, films or independent publications about *Star Wars*. Lucasfilm earned a reputation as a litigious company that sued non-enfranchised authors (*Publishers Weekly*, March 15, 1999). *The Science of Star Wars* (1999) by former NASA astrophysicist, Jeane Cavelos, was an exception that focused on the feasibility of the film's technology. Fearing legal action by "Darth Lucas," however, literary and scholarly studies of *Star Wars* are as rare as Jedi Knights.

Spirit of *Star Trek*

There are many technical studies of *Star Trek*: *The Physics* (Krauss 1996) *The Biology* (Andreadis 1999) and *The Computers* (Gresh and Weinberg 1999)— and none are licensed or endorsed by Paramount Studios. There are also humanist, literary, feminist and metaphysical treatments by independent scholars: *Enterprise Zones* (Harrison 1996); *The Meaning* (Richards 1997); *The Metaphysics* (Hanley 1998); *Race in Space* (Pounds 1999); *The Ethics* (Barad 2000); *The Human Frontier* (Barrett 2001); and *The Religions* (Porter 2000 and Kraemer 2001).

Star Trek (*The Original Series* 1966-1969) on television and at the movies, was a humanistic quest for knowledge. The difference between *Star Wars* and *Star Trek* (TOS) however, is evident in the mission statement of the *Starship Enterprise*: "To explore strange new worlds, to seek out new life and new civilizations, to boldly go where no man has gone before." It is true that Yoda says in *The Empire Strikes Back*, "A Jedi uses the Force for knowledge."

In *Star Trek* (TOS) like *Star Wars*, the action takes place in outer space — the "new community" according to Joseph Campbell. "The community today is the planet not the bounded nation," he wrote in 1949. In *Star Trek (TOS)* however, there are no prominent women players and little concern for the deeper meaning of life. The central rift is rational versus irrational differences among adventurous males who explore outer space.

Curious Males Probe Universe

The hero of *Star Trek (TOS)* is the logically minded, middle-aged, Captain Kirk (William Shatner) who is always in control but also compassionate and amorous. He is more thoughtful and play-ful than masculine role models of the past, i.e. Ronald Reagan. Still, James Tiberius Kirk is the decisive captain, on and off the bridge of his spaceship (classic symbol of curious males probing the universe).

At his right hand is Mister Spock (Leonard Nimoy) half irrational human (mother) and half rational Vulcan (father). Spock is admired precisely because he dominates the mother side, with the father side, of his mind. His emotions and inward conceptions of human liberation are repressed. Spock frequently overrides the sensitive physician, Doctor McCoy (DeForrest Kelley) and can contradict the captain within limits that respect these politics of the mind.

All I Really Need to Know I Learned Watching Star Trek (1994) was a best seller by Madison Avenue advertising executive, Dave Marinaccio. It concerned life lessons in becoming a successful businessman who deals with challenges, fights for justice, treats rivals fairly, remains professional and knows "how to pick up girls." About the cavalier Kirk, the author states, "He's always in fighting [and love making] shape. Kirk is a military man. His method of dealing with conflict is to confront it straight on."

Heroic Farm Boy

But *Star Wars* is the exact opposite: an innocuous, eighteen-year old boy gives up physical fighting and dedication to temporal power to become a mature, genderless "Jedi Knight." Mark Hamill was twenty-four years old when *Star Wars* began in 1975 and thirty-two

UNSPECTACULAR HEROES

George Lucas as a young man and Luke Skywalker (Mark Hamill) as a character in *Star Wars*, are unspectacular heroes who mirror one another in real life and in the movies. The two exemplify the idea that becoming a peace knight requires no special biographical, biological, racial or supernatural qualities and is an option for any ordinary person willing to initiate the process.

---

in 1983 when it ended, but he looks like a preteen in beginning *Episode IV*. The trilogy spans four years and there is a three-year gap between *Episode IV* and *V*, meaning that Luke was 21 in the former and 22 in the latter.

According to the annotated official script that includes all the scenes either cut or not filmed, Lucas first describes Luke Skywalker as "a farm boy with heroic aspirations who looks much younger than his eighteen years." His sister, Leia, on the other hand, is sixteen-years old and not yet a twin. Lucas himself was in his early thirties, just a scrawny young man in blue jeans, sneakers and thick-framed glasses, easily disregarded as film director.

As a guileless rube who becomes a great space hero, Mark Hamill was ingeniously cast. His small, youthful stature, *androgynous* appearance, physical awkwardness and personal insecurities are all factors that reveal weaknesses that run counter to the popular conception of the action hero. Luke is just an average young man — with no special abilities — one who grows up bored on a desert planet — dramatic devices that lend empathy to his character.

During casting, Mark Hamill said he thought Harrison Ford, who played Han Solo, was "the Flash Gordon character and I must be sidekicks." That Luke required more training as an actor, according to critics, revealed an immature figure of acute vulnerability

Sage of Ancient Wisdom

ANDROGENY: BISEXUAL APPEARANCE AND PERSONALITY NOT DIVIDED BY SEX ROLE SOCIALIZATION.

one of the with whom viewers identify. His image contrasts with that of his father in *Phantom Menace*, who plays boy wonder, electronic genius, champion pod-racer, military superhero and interplanetary savior, all as a mere child.

The ungainly Luke was an unlikely candidate for the role of valiant hero, just as a small, ugly, old, green, froglike, creature, with long pointed ears, as wide as his height, was an unlikely sage of wisdom. Lucas said he picked Hamill because "he was a gosh and golly kid which is what I wanted Luke to be" (Pollock 1990). Extraordinary deeds by the everyday person fascinate those who find life tedious. Divine descent belongs to simple folk like Forrest Gump.

Harrison Ford was a carpenter working on movie set construction when Lucas discovered him, first for a minor role in *American Graffiti* (Universal 1973) and later for the part of the rogue adventurer, Han Solo. About *Star Wars* Lucas said, "It's aimed primarily at teenagers, the same audience as *American Graffiti*." But, *Star Trek* (TOS) targeted middle-aged, upper middle-class, male professionals with discretionary income.

In *Star Wars* the truth is found ultimately within the self as opposed to the outer limits of the galaxy in *Star Trek*. This means *Star Wars* is focused on self-discovery, while *Star Trek* concerned excitement in researching outer space. A "trek" explores the universe, while a "war" within the self is reconciled by becoming a keeper of peace. The latter transforms personality while the former tries to extend its dominion everywhere.

Kathryn Janeway (Kate Mulgrew) took over the bridge of the *Star Trek Voyager* series (1995-2001). Themes and symbols from the three previous series, all under male command, were now altered. *Voyager* was still science fantasy television about a dedicated crew of men and women astronauts. But Janeway's team got lost, light years from earth in the "Delta Quadrant" of remote space. Metaphorically, this suggested that being cut off from a higher self is the basic human dilemma.

Star Trek = Mind Trek

In the two-part, opening episode, the fresh crew is swept suddenly in a space storm, like humans ripped from Heaven, 70,000 light years away by a powerful "Caretaker." A literary-philosophical study of *Star Trek* by Michèle and Duncan Barrett (2001) a British mother and son team, claim this was a dramatic device for looking back at earth and ourselves. "This voyage out is also a voyage in," they assert. Far away from home you are freer to examine yourself.

Poetry Explores Inner Space

"The exploration of the cosmos is a voyage of self-discovery," announced popular astronomer Carl Sagan (1934-1996) in his classic, thirteen-part drama, *Cosmos: A Personal Voyage*. This was the most watched public television series in history, seen by 500 million people in 60 countries and a book on the *New York Times* bestseller list for 70 weeks in the 1980s. Paradoxically, Sagan believed only matter and energy existed and was skeptical about faith based on institution or revelation.

Home in Your Mind

You do not have to go into orbit to find yourself. Reading and writing poetry are methods for exploring inner space — creatively locating wisdom at home on the range of your mind. The crew of *Voyager*, however, explores the galaxy and confronts hostile alien species. To settle disputes with strange new races and among the heterogeneous crew, Captain Janeway avoids using force, but it rarely works. Tricorder and computer scans diagnose most problems that are ultimately solved by erecting weapons shields and photon torpedo blasts.

An avowed atheist-scientist, Captain Janeway is depicted as an eccentric who uses intuition only as a practical last resort. "Do it" is an old *Star Trek* slogan she reiterates often to make change happen

Inner Space Research

along the way (echoing sea captains on classic sailing ships telling crews "to make it so"). Janeway's female officers are highly rational, i.e., the cybernetic Seven of Nine (Jeri Ryan) and the chief engineer B'Elanna Torres (Roxann Dawson).

The Vulcan, Tuvok (Tim Russ) does "mind melds" and Kes (Jennifer Lien) is a member of an intuitive species called the Ocampa. But her lifespan of nine years is cut short when she dies at age two to make way for the *deborged*, Seven of Nine. Kes was never admitted as a regular crewmember, unlike her replacement, who is Captain Janeway's darling. Using warp speed that takes twenty-three years, the company is exhausted and elderly when they finally return to earth, as are most earthlings by the time they go to faith (or die without it).

After seven seasons on the air, the series ends with Tuvok, tactical and security officer, dying of a degenerative neurological disorder that pathetically wipes out his mind. Janeway sacrifices her life to destroy the enemy Borg Queen and her Hive of assimilated *automatons*. The ending suggests that inner space research is far more treacherous to explore than outer space. The fifth series, *Star Trek: Enterprise* (2001) reinstates a male captain who hunts galactic terrorists that are plotting to destroy earth. Unlike *Star Wars*, there is no inward transformation to establish universal peace through nonviolent consciousness.

DEBORGED: RESCUED FROM THE BORG RACE WHO CONVERT SPECIES INTO AUTOMATONS. **AUTOMATONS**: MECHANIZED BEINGS.

The most spiritually oriented *Star Trek* film was *The Final Frontier* (1989) directed, written and starring William Shatner. Shot with the *TOS* cast, twenty years after the series ended, Kirk and Spock were fifty-eight and "Bones," the medical doctor, nearly seventy-years-old. A renegade Vulcan named Sybok (Laurence Luckenbill) is a telepathic healer and Spock's half-brother. In a literal quest to locate God outside the galaxy, Sybok rebels against all reason to space jack the *Enterprise*.

Going beyond the "great barrier reef" of fear, the men encounter a cruel and irate deity, a projection of Sybok, who destroys himself in dismay over his error. Staying rational and using their weapons, the crew escapes this demented fanatic in their newly outfitted spacecraft. Among fans and critics, *The Final Frontier* is the least popular *Star Trek* movie. The ending implies that having faith is insane. Rather, it is looking for God outside your mind that is absurd.

The tenth *Star Trek* film, *Nemesis* (2002) using *The Next Generation* cast, makes moral self-improvement the difference between good and bad human beings. Robots are not capable of understanding this distinction. Using doubles to reinforce the message, both Jean-Luc Picard, the captain (Patrick Stewart) and his science officer Data (Brent Spiner) encounter replicas who represent their shadow sides.

Picard faces a young villain copied from his own DNA, "Shinzon" (Tom Hardy) and Data encounters prototype "B4" (before). Both duplicates are defective. Shinzon degenerates neurologically and wants only to payback his miscreators while B4 was not programmed to learn, and can only imitate his clever master, Shinzon. Picard thinks that genuine human beings rise above their physical limitations, unlike these opponent-selves.

The two philosophies battle for supremacy and their spaceships collide. Data proves he has acquired the capacity to overcome *android* limitations by blasting the bad guys (and himself) to smithereens. This violent resolution, however, contradicts the captain's basic premise. Affected by shock waves perhaps, everyone acts like the good guys have won through virtue. Since nothing has changed inwardly, we are assured that clones of the dark side will rise again.

ANDROID: COMPUTERIZED ROBOT DESIGNED IN HUMAN FORM.

THREE

PARABLE OF FAITH

Inscribed in the *Star Wars* film series is a theology and cosmology — a set of basic principles about the nature of God, humankind and the universe. Master Jedi Knights Yoda and Obi-Wan Kenobi teach Luke Skywalker, a novice, that "the Force is what gives a Jedi his power. It surrounds us and penetrates us. It binds the galaxy together." Most audiences know that "the Force" is a spiritual power.

"The Force is a secularized version of God," wrote Matthew C. Mohs. Frank Allnutt authored the first evangelical Christian commentary on *Star Wars*, *The Force of Star Wars* (1977, 1999). "The true Force is Almighty God," he claimed and sold over 210,000 copies of his book (frankallnutt.com). David Wilkinson, British writer and Methodist minister, continues the theme in *The Power of the Force* (2000).

The history of Jedi Knights is recorded in the various *Star Wars* novels and serves as the backdrop to the galactic warfare that frames the two trilogies. The old league of Jedi Knights worshiped a power called "the Force" and was its moral custodians for fifty centuries. But an expert in belligerence, Emperor Palpatine and his second in command, Darth Vader, purge their reign.

Luke Skywalker reinforces the Jedi Knights and his call to adventure unites the series of six films into one epic drama. The hero is destined to save or damn humanity by choosing between the morality of his spiritual father, Obi-Wan Kenobi or the aspirituality of his biological father, Darth Vader. In finally electing faith, for all humanity, Luke relinquishes fighting forever.

A spiritual foundation in *Star Wars* exists whether the director intended it or not. In a *Playboy* magazine interview, George Lucas explained, "I was trying to say, in a simple way, that there is a God and that there is both a good side and a bad side. You have a choice between them . . ." (Weintraub 1997). According to inside reports (Jenkins 1997) Lucas was "adamant" about proposing a spiritual perspective though he repudiates this idea (pages 49 and 64).

In the annotated screenplays Lucas wrote, "I'm not dealing with deep psychological problems. My films are storytelling movies." But he is telling stories of another kind here because "the Force" was conceived as a common denominator to all religions — primitive to modern. The idea of an ideological core to world religion was a premise in the writings of Joseph Campbell, who Lucas once called, "My Yoda" (*Foreword*).

To call God "the Force" is no huge undertaking. But to abstract all religion into a single phrase is a hefty metaphysical task for a mere teller of (tall) tales. In a *Time Magazine* interview with Bill Moyers (April 1999) Lucas explained, "I consciously set about to recreate

GOOD AND BAD FORCES

Bill Moyers interviewed George Lucas concerning the "true theology of the Force" ("Of Myth and Men," *Time Magazine*, April 1999) "I would hesitate to call the Force God" said Lucas. They discuss life as a battle between good and evil forces that culminates in the tragedy and finality of death. Fighting evil, however, makes death appear awful and justifies attacks on enemies in the name of self-defense.

---

myths [with] classical motifs." And, "I didn't want to use God or any of those kinds of connotations. . . . I eventually shorthanded it just to the Force.

Like literary allegories of the past — Dante's *The Divine Comedy* and Homer's *The Iliad* and *The Odyssey*, for example, the normative narrative makes *Star Wars* a morality play. "Allegory" comes from the Greek language, meaning to speak figuratively about the hidden meaning that transcends the literal meaning of a text. In Judaism, for example, the body of the law, the *Torah*, is interpreted in the *Mishnah*, the spirit of the law.

Abstract Self-Conception

From the Greek word that gives us "to compare," parables in the Holy Bible are used to teach religious principles. *Star Wars* is thus a modern parable that communicates theological ideas in the form of entertainment. The ancient battle of the corporeal, versus the spiritual self, torn between good and evil, challenges us to look beyond literal perception to an abstract view of being spiritual.

The *Parable of Luke Skywalker* depicts a war between sacred and profane cosmic forces. Kevin M. Nord notes, "When young Skywalker's name is compressed into first name and last initial, it becomes 'Luke S.,' intensifying suspicion of this character as a

TORAH: SACRED SCRIPTURE OF JUDAISM AND FIRST FIVE BOOKS OF THE CHRISTIAN BIBLE.

directorial stand-in. This pivotal figure is perhaps a shortened form of 'Lucas.'" During filming, Mark Hamill said, "Oh, I see, of course, Luke is George" (Jenkins, 1997). Also, "Lucas," in Spanish, is Luke.

Parable of Faith

The oft-quoted opening crawl, "In a galaxy far, far away, a long time ago," is more time now than young people in the audience can remember. Yet, as Jonathan Young explains in the *Foreword*, this storytelling spans generations. It focuses on humanity several centuries into the future reviewing its history. Similarly, the prequels concern an earlier time nearer to our own. Henderson explains, "Lucas has taken a highly advanced technological society and portrayed it as existing in the past."

Thus, events on earth during the 20th Century are "prequel" to the six sequels of *Star Wars*, projected out as the future of the planet. *Star Trek* occurs in the Twenty-Fourth Century, whereas *Star Wars* takes place in the Twenty-Third. This means the focus of *Phantom Menace: Episode I*, lies immediately ahead in the Twenty-First or Twenty-Second Centuries (Chapter 10).

For the debut of *Phantom Menace*, Lucas said in promotional appearances that "*Star Wars* is just a movie," but at the same time he declared, "it was designed to make people think about the larger . . . mysteries of life" (Bob Heisler, "It's Just a Movie," *Los Angeles Times*, May 20, 1999.) Paul Lieberman reported that Lucas "also recalls how he set out originally to create nothing less than 'a modern mythology' " (*Los Angeles Times*, "*Star Wars* Gets Forceful Unveiling," May 10, 1999).

Star Wars & Star Peace?

For a movie with absolute non-violence as the solution to galactic mayhem, *Star Wars* is a one-sided title. Leo Tolstoy (1828-1910) called his classic epic, *War and Peace*. (It's just a title?) Lucas's hero goes beyond *satyagraha*, the passive resistance of Mohandas Gandhi (1869-1948) leader of India's national independence from two hun-

MYTHOLOGICAL INTENTION

I was trying to take certain mythological principles and apply them to a story. Ultimately, I had to abandon that and just simply write the story. I found that when I went back and read it, then started applying against the sort of principles that I was trying to work with originally, they were all there. It's just that I didn't put them in there consciously. I'd sort of immersed myself in the principles . . . [and] these things were just indelibly infused into the script.

George Lucas quoted in *The Magic of Myth*

---

dred years of British colonial rule. *Star Wars and Star Peace* might not fascinate audiences as a title, or draw commercially. Still, "moral philosopher" is Lucas's clandestine persona.

COSMIC HERO

Star Wars can be viewed as the action adventure of a superhero who battles good and evil in the universe. Or, the series of films may be seen as a struggle in the life of one person to gain wisdom and find peace of mind. In the second case, all the figures, places, objects and events concern the thinking of Luke, or Lucas, a representative human being who wants to become a wisdom hero who grasps the meaning of life.

Just as every cell in the human body contains the entire DNA sequence of an individual, every person is part of a greater mind. One person psychologically represents all people and "reality" is this inner self cast outward. "Every mind contains all minds for every mind is one"(ACIM). Movies thus can be read as projections, meaning all the characters that populate a story are psychic aspects common to all people.

I
am
Them

They
are
Me

We
are
One

Luke is an *archetype* — a model of the wisdom hero's thought system. Though the form may vary according to personal taste, cultural tradition and temporal period, Luke's pathway is one that anyone can follow in their spiritual evolution toward the Light. *Star Wars* thus reflects the inner battle of a cosmic figure, trustee for humanity at large, as he or she comes to comprehend the law of faith in God.

The fundamental law of faith states that every human being possesses Light in an innermost self, just like Luke Skywalker, and is an emissary of peace, just like the Jedi Knights. It is not possible to be outside the fateful law because God is omnipresent, omnipotent and omniscient — the first cause of all causes. In being aware of the link to the divine, "the world" can exist in relative harmony.

Darth Vader and Obi-Wan Kenobi stand for protagonist and antagonist, competitors for dominance in the split mind of the mortal Luke. Darth Vader dispossesses himself of the Force on account of some great tragedy in his past and tries to take over his son's thinking with military might. *Phantom Menace* reveals his experience as young Anakin Skywalker; how warfare broke out in his mind and in the galaxy simultaneously (Chapter 10).

Obi-Wan Kenobi, on the other hand, possesses the power of consciousness and appeals to Luke to recognize a shared identity through faith in an inner connection to the Force. The central struggle is the one for supremacy over thinking — to which side will Luke turn — to the genetic law that he is the biological son or to the cosmic law of faith that he is the spiritual son? Which rules his destiny?

Impulsive, aggressive and arrogant, these two figures resemble one another, like halves of a whole, but are dramatized as separate actors who are actually facets of a single person. They act like brothers

ARCHETYPE: BASIC MODEL, IDEAL TYPE, TEMPLATE.

who join opposing armies during historical civil wars. Psychologically, they represent human beings with split identities, according to the reign of lower versus higher consciousness in their thinking.

"Obi-Wan Kenobi and Darth Vader started as one character in the screenplay until Lucas separated them into the good and bad fathers," according to Lucas's biographer Dale Pollock (1990). Actually, three characters inhabit the mind: Luke is the conscious self, Darth Vader the secular self and Obi-Wan the sacred self. Typically, we are divided three ways: who we think we are and whom others think we are, two versions of the false-self and who we truly are as spiritual beings.

Who Rules Destiny?

Luke's dilemma resembles that of Cain in *Genesis*, who also was conceived before but born after Adam and Eve were expelled from the grace of the Garden of Eden. Just as Cain, the bad son, follows his father, Adam, in the providential lack of faith, Luke fears he will imitate his father's tumble through heaven's gate. The story of the Garden of Eden can also be read psychologically. Cain "killing" Abel is lower consciousness taking over higher consciousness — a common mortal mishap.

Luke's relationship with Leia also may be seen as a self-relationship, to his "sister-self" instead of his "brother-self." Twin emphasizes identicality. Luke's "contra-sexual self" has many literary names: "anima," "psyche," "soul" and "inner feminine being." Leia stands for the mythological figure, "Holy Sophia," from whom we get "philosophy," the love of knowledge. She guides the inward journey to faith in a transcendent second half of life.

Humans with Split Identities

The cast of good and bad characters (crewmen, robots, bounty hunters) represent angelic and demonic aspects in the intrapsychic life of regular people. Making its mystical presence felt in consciousness, Jedi Knights, for example, symbolize the intelligent and crea-

Spiritual Computers?

In the struggle against the Empire, the droids do not have the potential to be violent in any meaningful way. C-3PO never comes close to violence and R2-D2 struggles almost playfully with Yoda and an Ewok, both unassuming and unthreatening creatures. Both droids wind up having to be repaired in all three movies because they have been damaged or virtually destroyed in an act of violence beyond their means of defense.

They rely upon the intervention of Luke, Han, Leia, or Chewbacca to rescue them or repair them. . . . unable to be violent and faced with an opponent unwilling to communicate, the droids wind up as a pile of scrap. Their inability to be violent, however, does not render them useless. At some point within each film, C-3PO and R2-D2 manage to save the day because of their ability to communicate, either with other people or other machines. C-3PO with his knowledge of six million forms of communication acts as translator and medium for the Alliance throughout the trilogy.

In 'Return of the Jedi,' his mastery of language convinces the Ewoks to join in the struggle against the Empire — an important turning point in the film. R2-D2's capacity to interface with other machines and computers allows Luke to finish his successful attack on the Death Star, fixes the deactivated hyperdrive on the Millennium Falcon averting almost certain capture and gives Luke his light sabre on Jabba's barge allowing him to complete the rescue of Han Solo.

Matthew C. Mohs

tive capacities of the hidden self that seek, in concert, an alternative to psychic pain and universal turmoil. The cosmic hero is thus an ordinary person.

Like Holy Sophia, Yoda represents ancient wisdom buried deep in the psyche of human beings, but being less evolved than she, he appears in animal form. Holy Sophia assists the Godhead, but takes a human form. When Lucas conceived of Yoda, he had read Joseph Campbell (1949) who wrote, "In fairy lore it may be some little fellow of the wood, some wizard, hermit, shepherd or smith, who appears to supply *amulets* and advice the hero will require."

Cosmic Hero = Ordinary Mortal

Yoda appears to be an irascibly flawed little creature who actually is a split-off and overlooked part of our own mind that can be reintegrated to recognize the wisdom of the ancient masters. Yoda corresponds to the "inner wizard" in the mortal mind, according to what Merlin the Magician taught young King Arthur (Chopra 1995). As a sage, Yoda too evolves from the prequels to the sequels.

Inward Journey to Faith

In *The Wizard of Oz* (MGM 1939) a farm girl of indistinct age from the Midwest (Judy Garland) is swept away by a cyclone to the Land of Oz. In the book (1899) she actually makes the trip, but in the film she goes in a dream after being knocked unconscious. Dorothy encounters rural folk, good and bad witches and three memorable characters: Lion, Tin Man and Scarecrow. In this unique Americn fairy tale, a female hero rescues three troubled males.

Dorothy is lost and her companions lack brains, heart and courage, qualities we are told they really possess. The males in turn help rescue Dorothy from the wicked Witch of the West who is dissolved with plain water. The author, L. Frank Baum, was influenced by feminism and *theosophy*. Dorothy knew she needed help to get back home, though no one had ever seen a wizard before.

AMULET: TANGIBLE REMINDER OF FAITH USUALLY WORN AND INSCRIBED. **THEOSOPHY:** ANCIENT SPIRITUALITY BASED ON MYSTICAL INSIGHT AND METAPHYSICAL MOVEMENT IN THE U. S. IN THE LATE 19TH CENTURY LED BY HELENA PEROVNA BLAVATSKY.

vises sensible faith, obvious logic in *following the yellow brick road* and is not dissuaded despite many obstacles along the way.

Four Pilgrims to Oz

There is a common answer as Dorothy guides the pilgrims to Emerald City. The wizard offers token amulets, a diploma for the Scarecrow, for example, to protect against his incapacitating and recurring self-doubt. The Lion (facing danger) and the Tin Man (having passion) are emotions also necessary for success in life. Baum's biographer claims they were given the "self-confidence to recognize their own worth" (Rogers 2002).

The fraternal twin robots, Artoo Detoo and See-Threepio (aka R2-D2 and C-3PO) are exemplars of the potential to remain steadfast comrades in open communication while exercising nonviolent options. Their irritability and bickering, however, depict their human-like frailty in this endeavor. Ironically, it is the adroit droids who tap into the mystical force and rise above ordinary human beings through having rational faith.

The computers lack the guilt associated with bodily functions that allows them to take the incremental steps — to be logical and faithful at the same time. Having faith in a relationship of mutual trust with each other and the Force is rational, and by comparison, human beings are disturbed most of the time. Anger is always the projection of guilt produced by self-condemnation in being alienated from God that justifies attacks on others as self-defense.

Logical & Faithful

Because rational faith terrifies us, the odd robotic pair is depicted as comics who compare to Laurel and Hardy, *el gordo y el flaco*. Artoo Detoo is the short "chrome dome," with his sidekick, See-Threepio, a golden robot with one silver leg who resembles a life-size Oscar. According to Lucas, the pair did not receive a warm welcome, in the same way that Jar Jar Binks in *Phantom Menace* wrangled the nerves of fans and critics.

The robotic odd couple, C-3P0 and R2-D2, are incapable of violence and revenge. Transcending human limitation, they remain steadfast in rational devotion to the Force. They are continuously assaulted and dismantled by humans envious and threatened by their superior spiritual capacity. The two represent models to be emulated.

Wisdom Hero

In *The Empire Strikes Back*, the recruit to wisdom is a young fighter pilot who joins the revolt against the overwhelming forces of an evil empire. Luke wants to become a special warrior to defeat the enemy commander of death, "Lord Darth Vader," a contraction perhaps of Dark Invader and Death Father. He is the demonic head of one-world government, the pope of anti-hope, the supreme hater in the galaxy.

In Christian theology, Luke is in the service of the Lord to save humanity by becoming an Archangel in order to rid the world of Satanic rule. Being an emissary of God and validating the good in every person, his conversion to the religion of the Jedi Knights takes place the moment he sees that he bears the Force. This power remains latent in him and invisible to others, however, as long as he is cloaked in aggression.

In the *New Testament*, Jesus, the Son of Man, is christened to become Jesus, the Son of God, while in *Star Wars*, Luke, the son of Darth Vader, is knighted to become the son of Yoda and Obi-Wan. Like the children of Adam and Eve, Luke and his twin sister Leia, were conceived before, but born after their father defected to the "dark side." Luke saves or damns humanity according to whether he honors his biological or spiritual father.

Cloaked in Aggression

Emperor Palpatine and his second officer resemble historical rulers like the Roman Emperor Caesar Tiberius and his local governor Pontius Pilate, two levels of an alien power structure during the Roman occupation of Judea. Jesus of Nazareth appears to teach spiritual principles to an inner circle of disciples and speaks of the eternal love of a deity who subordinates life to moral principles as do Yoda and Obi-Wan in *Star Wars*.

In an oral tradition, Jesus teaches the apostles to believe in an inner kingdom that is broadcast through the "good news" of the gospels. He tells them in their first meeting as a group and to the multitudes gathered to hear the *Sermon on the Mount* that they know from the Law of Moses, "Thou shalt not kill," but he adds that it makes no sense even to get angry (*Matthew* 5:21).

Palpatine was an innocuous figure who promised reforms in government during the demise of the old order. His unassuming manner helped him to gain power in that he appeared not to pose a threat to anybody, but soon, he became tyrannical. Luke's training is imperative to save rebel civilization from annihilation by the superior technology and greater numbers of the invader.

Anger Makes No Sense

The proclaimed warlord, together with his venal accomplice, sweeps away the remnants of the past, fights the incipient rebellion and launches a genocidal holocaust. Despite their standing as a force of good for thousands of years, the moral knights lose their hold on the universe. Unbounded greed and ruthless corruption take over, resembling the decline of Canaan, Palestine in ancient times, destroyed by the great flood of Noah's time.

Jedi Knights are "almost extinct" due to the "seductive power" of the forbidden "dark side." Luke repeatedly is warned "not to underestimate the power of the dark side of the Force." The means of

TWIN SELF

Separated at birth, Luke and Leia Skywalker are potential peace knights but do not know one another nor their father who is the leader of evil in the galaxy. They represent the primary division of the self into masculine and feminine personalities by a polarized world at war with evil. Trained in consciousness, however, they can be restored to wholeness and end all strife. That Leia was never trained means the task is left unfinished at the conclusion of *Star Wars*.

Means of Seduction

seduction are the belief in the reality of enemies and attacks based on emotions like fear, anger and hate. Yoda's instantly classic line, played up in the advertising trailer for *Phantom Menace*, was: "Fear leads to anger . . . anger leads to hate . . . hate leads to suffering."

Lucas once explained that "having machines like the droids that are reasonably compassionate and a man like Vader who becomes a machine and loses his compassion, was a theme that interested me." Mechanicals act human and humans act mechanical in the *Star Wars* empire, but the good side is only obscured, not eliminated. Because humans envy their ability of rational faith, the two robots are quirky eccentrics.

One Wayward Knight

Darth Vader is the anti-Christ and Obi-Wan Kenobi is his failed instructor in knighthood. Darth Vader was a Jedi Knight in training who fell from grace (like Lucifer from Heaven). Trying to save him from the "dark side," Obi-Wan accidentally knocked him into a lava pit that completed his anti-baptism. Darth Vader became a killing machine, hell bent on destruction. Judging by the size of his fury, he must have fallen into a volcano. One wayward knight then menaces the entire universe with hatred.

Twin Stars = Dual Destiny

Darth Vader emerged mutilated and degenerated into the jaded Jedi Knight. To survive, he required technological life support systems, which are installed in a private chamber. He breathes and speaks through a mechanical device and cannot live without his mask and helmet, described by Lucas as "a walking iron lung." His heavy breathing is considered sinister but actually is symptomatic of some infirmity like asthma or emphysema. He speaks in a low, powerful voice supplied by James Earl Jones.

Luke Skywalker and his twin sister, Leia Organa, were born eighteen years before *A New Hope*. The same year their father turned evil, but he was not aware of their birth. Luke's mentor, Obi-Wan Kenobi, thought Anakin's fall was fatal and when he found out he survived as Darth Vader, to protect the minors as targets of reprisal, he relocated Luke to one planet and Leia to another, with their mother, Queen Padmé Amidala-Skywalker.

Neither child was informed of their birthright (or birth wrong). Leia was brought up in a royal foster family on a peaceful planet and was known as Princess Leia. She did not know she had a twin brother. Though Leia remembered her mother, Padmé's disappearance remained mysterious until her murder is revealed in *Revenge of the Sith* (Chapter 10). The diminutive Leia became a galactic senator, but she also secretly joined her foster father as a leader in the army of rebellion.

Luke was sent to a remote planet that had the distinction of two suns blazing side by side in the sky. The climate was inhospitable and the terrain hued double orange in color. The twin stars were signs of the heavenly destiny of brother and sister in restoring enlightenment to the galaxy. Two brilliant stars indicate that wisdom knights of peace can belong to either gender. Standing on the horizon before the setting suns, Luke is described by Matthew C. Mohs:

> *Lucas shoots Luke in extreme long shot from behind with the suns in the background — a technique that isolates his hero with the horizon, much like a scene from an old western. He then cuts to a medium shot to capture the expressions on Luke's face as he contemplates his future.*

Like young King Arthur (Spider-Man, Dorothy of Oz and Muhammad of Islam) Luke was raised in obscurity by his aunt and uncle, and knew little about the fate of his real parents. The wisdom hero may be an orphan who has no natural parents, but human beings are never abandoned by God. Earthly conditions are totally irrelevant to spiritual inheritance.

Two Reclusive Sentinels

Obi-Wan's bitter brother, Uncle Owen, resembling the "good son" in the biblical parable of the *Prodigal Son*, obediently stayed down on the farm while the younger brother wandered the galaxy. Obi-Wan was trained as a Jedi Knight, learned about the Force from Master Yoda, served as a general in galactic civil wars, defended the old order and retreated to become Luke's guardian.

Obi-Wan and Yoda are reclusive sentinels in a morally waning universe who live in seclusion as the last hope to overthrow the new reign of corruption. "Ben Kenobi" is known locally as an eccentric old hermit. He resides near his brother to oversee Luke's upbringing, waiting to train him when Luke comes of age. This is unlike Merlin the Magician, who actually took over the parenting of young King Arthur (Chapter 4).

Converted to The Force

As an act of redemption for his error, Obi-Wan becomes Luke's guardian and is martyred at the end of the trilogy. Young man Luke is a heroic figure who prevents a vast, climactic battle between good and evil by converting himself and his father to the Force at the close of the six-act drama. For Luke, the struggle is between Obi-

Wan Kenobi, his spiritual father, and Anakin Skywalker, his biological father, also known as Darth Vader.

One Peace Knight

Luke learns that the eradication of terrorists, even for peace and justice, is futile. The conclusion shows that you can be misguided all your life and still fulfill your destiny. Luke comes to understand that fighting for any reason is mistaken and he lays down his arms. Two trilogies set up the revelation that occurs during the last moments of *Return of the Jedi*. That is, "Star Peace" is the result of a decision to be absolutely non-violent and is the ultimate moral lesson of *Star Wars*.

Until the climax, Luke's mind is divided between two characters, Darth Vader, the anti-Christ, and the spiritually loyal Obi-Wan Kenobi. Rather than being purged as the last living Jedi Knight, however, Luke expels the idea that "evil" exists in him, or in anyone in the galaxy. Only recognition, not aggressive or defensive action, restores the universe to good. The personal peace of one knight then saves humanity from all future warfare and eliminates evil in the world.

MYSTICAL BEING

Yin & Yang of Taoism

According to Jonathan Young (1999) when the hero is advised to "trust in the Force," a mystical power is evoked. John Porter, in *The Tao of Star Wars* (2003) among others, has noted the similarities in the idea of the Force in *Star Wars* and the polar energies of Yin and Yang in the ancient Eastern religion of Taoism.

Star Wars characters also resemble archetypes in the collective unconscious described by Carl. G. Jung. There are, for example: the Shadow, the Wise Old Man, the Dwarf, the Trickster and other figures. The influences of the psychoanalyst Jung and the mythologist Joseph Campbell on the *Star Wars* films is discussed by Young in the *Foreword* to this book.

A life-energy in Hinduism is known as *Jeeva* and in Tai Chi Chuan martial arts it is called *Chi*. Mediaeval alchemists described a vital force named the *Spiritus Mundi*. As an "energy field," however, the Force sounds more remote and electric, than mystic and deistic. Han Solo exclaims, "There's no mystical energy field that controls my destiny."

Mystic & Diestic

The idea that God dwells intimately in the mind of every person is a doctrine in the West known as "mysticism." The more you cast your mind outward, however, the greater is the separation of the individual from the Source, into a material world of appearances where God appears to be absent. To mystics, the human mind personalizes the Mind of God, who is also universal.

Through introversion of the psyche, meditation and revelation are two direct ways to know God. Various charismatic movements in the past have returned God to the mind, but the idea became heretical during the European Middle Ages because it made the formal church irrelevant to salvation. As a result, an inner spiritual tradition was lost in the West until recently (Amis 1995).

Spiritual prescience (foreknowledge) is an idea honored also in Hinduism and Buddhism, i.e., "Krishna consciousness" and "Buddha nature." In Hinduism, "Brahma" means the awareness of God. According to legend, Buddha's last words were, "Be a light unto yourself." Christianity considers sin the absence of God and the New Testament proclaims the "Kingdom of God is within" (*Luke*: 17:21).

The Way of The Force

Many religions may have influenced the nebulous idea of the Force in *Star Wars*: Eastern Taoism, Western Mysticism, Hinduism, Buddhism and Christianity. To use labels like "Christian," "Hindu," "Jew" and "Muslim," however, can segregate us from the greater truth that there are many pathways to higher consciousness. God arising from different creeds can serve to unite rather than divide humanity. Luke is variously: *Wisdom Hero, Cosmic Hero, Archetype, Mystical Being and Ordinary Mortal.*

Many Paths to Consciousness

The message of *Star Wars* is not encrypted, but the adventure story's images and special-effects technology do shroud a sacred point of view. Though we are not deceived on purpose, audiences remain naive about the film's essential spiritual content. When the truth is rediscovered, however, Jedi Knights are no longer "extinct" via consignment to the individual unconscious.

Star Wars portrays the spirit of God existing within the depths of the human mind. The filmmaker himself was not fully aware of the mystical implications of what he created, nor that we are all of One Mind. Whether or not Lucas intended a spiritual message is irrelevant, since the message is the message, regardless of the director's intention. Lucas has said repeatedly, "I don't see *Star Wars* as profoundly religious."

The mystery of the holy Force in *Star Wars* is more familiar to the audience, however, than the many strange creatures and weird planets that provide entertainment. When awe struck by technological finesse, viewers may not recognize the film's spiritual foundation. Individuals partake at their own level of readiness. Audiences might not have put daily life aside to be immersed in this fantastic new vision had the message been more overtly theological.

FOUR

KING ARTHUR

This chapter traces the quest for spiritual consciousness through various historical, literary and mythological sources. The endeavor may involve a discussion of symbolism too abstract for some readers. The theme is taken up in popular science fiction film in Chapter 5. You can skip ahead and then return to read Chapter 4 as the next to last chapter of the book.

The Myth of King Arthur of Great Britain extends into the mist of prehistory. The classic telling of the tale is Sir Thomas Malory's famous *Morte d'Arthur*, written while he was imprisoned in London during the War of the Roses (1455-1486). The drawing on the next page by Aubrey Beardsley is taken from his book, *The Birth, Life and Acts of King Arthur* (London: J. M. Kent 1894) published originally in 1485.

HISTORY & MYTHOLOGY

		MIDDLE AGES	MODERN
RANKS OF KNIGHTS		Knave	Novice
		Page	Apprentice
		Esquire	Disciple
		Knight	Master

Battle of the Mind

The legend begins with a fratricidal rivalry in heaven between archangelic brothers, Michael and Lucifer, over loyalty to their Father. Accursed in defeat, Lucifer is cast out headlong and loses a glorious emerald from his crown, emblem of his soul that plummets into the abyss of the material world below. When this fallen angel is restored to his Father's house, sin will disappear for all humanity and earth will ascend unto heaven.

The Holy Grail is the acclaimed cup that Jesus Christ and his disciples passed around at the Last Supper. In mythology, it came to be associated with the golden chalice sought by King Arthur and his court castled at Camelot. In time, it was linked also with the cup that Joseph of Arimathea used to collect the blood, sweat and tears of Jesus at the crucifixion on Golgotha.

Grail Quest Seeks Soul

The Knights of the Round Table (and the Jedi Knights of the Force) seek Lucifer's lost soul that represents humanity's missing spiritual identity. In recovering the Holy Grail, the soul is spared the battle of the mind where guilt over sin rages between good and evil. The Holy Grail thus represents the capacity to stay aware of God, to forgive yourself and to see good in every person.

As adventurers, King Arthur and his knights mistook the sacred cup for a real object and imbued it with magical power. Likewise, *Jason and the Argonauts* sought a "golden fleece" and early drafts of *Star Wars* hunted a "Kyber Crystal." The Grail, Fleece and Crystal are tangible reminders to stay steadfast while seeking the love of

Young King Arthur

God. Like the "alchemical stone," "elixir of élan vital" or "holy water," these objects stand for the vitality of faith.

According to myth, King Arthur had to remove a sword locked inside a cold-anvil and hard-rock to be recognized as king of Great Britain. In the war against evil, the rock and anvil represent the sheathe of the mind when encased by guilt in cold and hard reality. The freed sword is discernment, through spiritual vision, of an alternative to using physical coercion.

Vitality of Faith

A sword traditionally is both a weapon of war and a symbol of authority. But a "light saber" suggests "knowing the light" and refers to the intelligence (sharp blade) that discerns mind power. The possession of the brilliant instrument enlightens you with the wit to wield the cutting edge of consciousness. As a result, you can rest comfortably at peace in inner and outer space.

Cutting Edge of Consciousness

Willing Right Hand & Arm

Finding the Holy Grail secures the lost soul that ends personal and social strife. In Beardsley's drawing, young King Arthur stands unarmed at the water's edge, saluting the Lady of the Lake in a gesture of respect. The exposed blade of her sword represents power in conventional external terms. But she offers him "Excalibur," the special sword of wisdom that lies hidden in the mind, like her submerged figure.

The pool reflects Arthur's consciousness at the start of the quest when knowledge is superficial. His figure appears to be feminine and his impending transformation is anticipated in his curvaceous shape, wide hips, breasts and delicate armor, all suggestive of the feminine dimension in human liberation. His salute demonstrates readiness to take the plunge and to join the masculine with the feminine side of his thinking.

The Lady of the Lake pricks his interest in finding spiritual empowerment with his mind. Piercing the upper world, the sword marks the point of decision to delve into the innermost realm. Willfully, Arthur raises his right hand and arm, signaling that he is ready to divest himself of worldly might, in exchange for enlightenment that lies beneath the surface.

Beacon to Inner Freedom

Like the Statue of Liberty in New York Harbor, holding aloft the torch of political freedom, the Lady of the Lake offers King Arthur a beacon to his true self. He confirms, by his attention and gesture, a willingness to dive for wisdom and undergo a personal transformation. His right hand turns skeletal as he begins symbolically to accept death of the body.

In legend, however, reverting to physical conquest, Sir Lancelot's illicit extramarital affair with Queen Guinevere brings down the entire kingdom. When the king lay mortally wounded at the hand of his own son, the black knight, Modred, he ordered the faithful

Sir Bedivere to return the sword to the lake because all the violent turmoil disregarded *the point* of spiritual mind power. An arm arose from the depths of the lake, brandished it three times, indicating misuse and disappeared.

The Point of Mind Power

The English actor Sir Alec Guinness (1914-2000) played the role of Obi-Wan Kenobi in *Star Wars*. Though he was born illegitimate, the British Crown knighted him in the 1950s. As a concession to 20th Century Fox Studios, Lucas chose Sir Alec as a celebrity to improve box office sales. Obi-Wan was "killed" in the conclusion to *A New Hope: Episode IV,* but reappeared as a "ghost" in *Episodes V and VI*.

The media reported during filming that Guinness was furious about his demise, but the actor claimed that he persuaded Lucas to kill-off his character. According to rumors, photographs of Obi-Wan sent by fans to Guinness for autographs, were thrown away by the actor. In his autobiography, *A Positively Final Appearance* (1999) he states, "I shrivel inside each time it [*Star Wars*] is mentioned" and "it has led to a worldwide taste for a fantasy world of secondhand, childish banalities."

Guinness enhanced the role of Obi-Wan Kenobi, the wise old man in the sea of space, making him less eccentric and nobler in character. He was just "a shabby old desert rat of a man," in Lucas' screenplay. (Facing his greatest peril upon returning home, Odysseus, in Homer's *The Odyssey*, disguised himself as an old beggar). Guinness was nominated for an academy award as best supporting actor for his performance in *Star Wars*.

Poor Old Beggar

HELEN OF TROY

Geographic Adventure = Metaphysical Quest

A big question in metaphysics is whether people are basically good, like their Creator, or sinful, guilty and fallible like their biological parents. According to the Holy Bible, God created man and woman in His "image." The question about human nature, therefore, cannot be answered apart from the larger issue — whether God is basically good or evil. If God is good, how do we account for imperfection and affliction in the world?

The search for the meaning of life has preoccupied scholars and explorers throughout the ages, and been an underlying motive for territorial conquest. In literature, the search for God is often portrayed as seeking after a unique woman and ultimately consecrated as a sacred marriage. The pursuit begins geographically, but due to hazards and failures along the way, the adventurer turns to philosophical concerns.

A blind visionary, Homer was the first great poet, composer of *The Iliad* and its sequel, *The Odyssey*, the two oldest works in Western literature. In the 8th Century B.C., he wrote of events that occurred 500 years earlier. In *The Iliad*, Odysseus seeks Helen and in *The Odyssey* he returns to his beloved wife Penelope. Dante searches for Beatrice in *The Divine Comedy* and Cupid adores Psyche in Roman folklore. A yearning for spiritual union is evident when symbolic meaning is given to these female figures.

In Greek myth, Helen is the daughter of Zeus, King of the Gods and Leda, a mortal, the most beautiful woman in the world. She marries Menelaus, King of Sparta, a city in Greece. In an abuse of hospitality, Paris, a Trojan prince from a rival state, abducts Helen to an ancient city in Asia Minor, now Turkey, known then as Troy. To rescue her, Menelaus and his older brother, Agamemnon, organize an expedition that includes famous warriors like Ajax and Achilles.

HISTORY & MYTHOLOGY

Homer chronicles the siege and defeat of Troy by Odysseus, known as Ulysses to the Romans. He offered a giant wooden horse as a great gift and when the gates open, the Spartans attack the Trojan city. *The Illiad* focuses on the military campaign, that is, on the sieges and assaults that occupy young men during their days of vigor and valor. Conquest is an ancient method for filling an existential void in the absence of faith.

Middle Years Wrestle Inner Demons

In *The Odyyssey*, after victory in the Trojan War, Odysseus heads home to Ithaca, a rocky isle off the coast of Greece, to live in peace as king with his wife, Penelope, and their son Telemachus. But on the way, he encounters attacks by the giant, one-eyed, man-eating Cyclops; seductions by the enchantress Circe, who turns men into pigs; and confinement by Calypso on her paradise isle. Cursed by Poseidon, god of the sea (the unconscious) he is tempted off-course by the songs of the Sirens (sexuality).

The sailors resist the Siren's call, but the ten-year return voyage is more treacherous than the outbound journey. Smoldering since youth and ignited by the fury over aging, deeper issues erupt as men and women reach middle years and wrestle with "inner demons." The Cyclops, for instance, may be regarded as the legacy of infantile egotism that sees the world from the point of view of one big eye centered in the forehead. The same design represents an inner eye of wisdom in Buddhism.

Or Find an Inner Eye?

When youthful triumphs prove inadequate against the onslaught of aging, hidden emotional conflicts rise to the surface during the second half of life. Circe and Calypso stand for aspects of the personality that hold back development during middle age. Both trick the person to stay stuck in a physical realm of consciousness, the former by seduction and the latter by entrapment. Odysseus defeats Circe and forces her to unenchant his crew. But afterwards, they stay a long time feasting and growing lazy.

Thus, *The Iliad* may be read as the trip out (physical conquests of young adulthood) and *The Odyssey* as the trip back (spiritual resolution of the crisis of midlife) during an indenture on earth. A similar story occurs in an earlier Greek myth, *Jason and the Argonauts*, who sailed for twenty years (their entire youth) searching for a golden fleece. Hera, Queen of the Gods, intervenes with Zeus, King of the Gods, to aid Jason and his crew of fifty sailors.

Onslaught of Aging

A film version directed by Don Chaffey (Columbia 1963) used stop-motion special effects by Ray Harryhausen to portray the demons. Loosely based on the myth, Jason encounters a giant bronze warrior, Talos, a venomous seven-headed serpent, Hydra, and seven in©destructible, sword-wielding skeletons. With the help of Medea, sorceress-daughter of a local king, Jason obtained the fleece. She becomes his lover (film) and wife (myth). The film-adventure ends at midpoint, but the voyagers return home in the legend.

HOLY SOPHIA

In mythology, the female form can represent both temptation and divine inner wisdom. Strongmen like Atlas and Hercules, Superman and Batman, stand for physical power in the phenomenal world. The Greek word "philo," meaning "love," coupled with the female name "Sophia," comprise "philosophy" and refer to the *love of knowledge*. Suggesting oneness, "psyche" means both mind and soul in Greek. "Sophia" is thus a female figure in mythology who personifies wisdom.

Guide to Inner Wisdom

As noted by Kevin M. Nord, when Luke Skywalker's first name and last initial are compressed, it reads, "Luke S." Nord suggests that "Luke" may be a condensed form of "Lucas," as in "George Lucas," and that the character represents the author and director of the *Star Wars* saga. But "Luke S." might also be spelled "Lukess" and in this case, we have a female "Jedi Knight" or "Holy Sophia."

FEMALE KNIGHTS

Princess Leia plants stolen blueprints of the enemy fortress in the computer R2-D2 who stands stoutly at attention and resolutely makes delivery to the rebel fortress. The plans lead to the destruction of the empire of evil and to the liberation of rebel humanity. Leia represents Holy Sophia, a female figure in mythology who serves as an inner guide for men and women to find the wisdom of faith.

Princcess Leia in *Star Wars* (and Trinity in *The Matrix*) represent the goddess who bears the truth that the spiritual quest lies within the breast of the innermost self. This remains true even though the characters are often embroiled in the fiercest fighting, side-by-side with the avenging males. Trained by her stepfather in martial arts to be a fighter, Leia solves conflict with violence just like real men.

Holy Sophia Personifies Wisdom

Luke's twin sister, his female counterpart, suggests that the whole person has no gender identity. She orders Artoo Detoo to deliver the stolen blueprints of the enemy fortress to the rebel forces and makes possible the explosion of its core. Thus, a woman and a robot persevere against all odds to demonstrate that logic and faith work together for higher causes. Based on an inner fitting, science and religion coordinate well when worn together as an outfit.

That "only" women (or men) are spiritual leaders is ridiculous, however, because both genders are notorious fighters. Leia's role is symbolic and stock photographs show her lethally armed. "Guide" refers to a feminine dimension in thinking, not to real women. As another example, Mary Magdala (Magdalene) was the "apostle to the apostles" in early Christianity (King 2003). But men and women both are vicious fighters when threatened by death without faith.

Logic & Faith

Divine Inner Wisdom

The genitals are regarded by society as powerful in terms of species reproduction. In mythology, however, the female figure represents inner power while the male figure stands for power in the physical world. Sophia leads us to the spiritual Mother-Father because she possesses the divine inner wisdom that an inseparable link to God always exists in the mind. As the mother of divine knowledge, she guides our return home through consciousness.

Both women and men seek transport by the archetype of the wise woman of the psyche. When consciousness is projected, however, Sophia is confined to obscurity in the unconscious, the way the Lady of the Lake remains submerged. Via female leadership (Lady of the Lake, Sophia, Leia) however, the way to the Light is revealed in the inbound connection to the Self. No matter where you are geographically, you are always in the right place spiritually.

As action heroes, males negotiate in the material world where survival depends on dexterity and strength. Films like *Terminator 3* (Warner Brothers 2003) emphasize muscle power and revenge. The ability to reproduce, however, is also associated with the mother due to the differential contribution of women to reproduction. To compensate, we are named after our father under the laws of patriarchy. The mother is also associated with spiritual birth but remains nameless here too.

Wise Woman of the Psyche

Historically, a cross indicates four basic directions. Before Christianity, in Egypt, the cross was surmounted by a loop, known as an "Ankh" or "Anch" (key of life) that resembles a human figure with outstretched arms. A Celtic cross encircles the center. Circle and loop imply femaleness (and the life cycle). The upper, round, feminine half tops the lower, linear, masculine half. Papal and patriarchal crosses, however, have horizontal beams indicating division and rank in society.

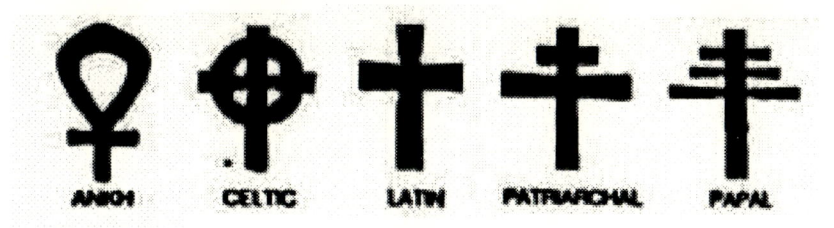

Types of Crosses

ANKH · CELTIC · LATIN · PATRIARCHAL · PAPAL

Holy Sophia is a guide to wisdom within the innermost self. When prospective peace knights of either gender pursue her affection, the relationship creates rapture. As an aroused lover, Lady Wisdom desires you too, and takes you when you are ready to follow her lead (Bergesen 2000). She offers the solace of intimate communion with God, just as Beatrice and Helen are soulful spouses to their poetic suitors. In vulgar versions, however, men seek Sophia as a carnal lover.

Inner Guide to Wisdom

Just before his death, Johann Wolfgang von Goethe (1749-1832) finished his epic poem, *Faust*, written over a sixty-year period, with the couplet, "Eternal Womanhead leads us on high." (*Das Ewig Weibliche/Zieht uns hinan*). A bond with God is also epitomized in the poetry of the Spanish priest, San Juan de la Cruz (1515-1591) in his classic *Dark Night of the Soul*. The writings of the Mexican nun, Sor Juana Inés de la Cruz (1651-1695) represent Holy Sophia in Latin American literature.

Yoda Not Yodo

The tender love of the mother mediates between the wayward child and the strict discipline of the father in the traditional family. Leia in *Star Wars* and Trinity in *The Matrix* are *anima* figures of young women who facilitate personal transformation by leading novices to the mastery of spirit. Due to her inner location, however, it is not necessary to undertake an actual journey in the outer world. The name "Yoda" also suggests a feminine persona.

ANIMA: LIFE-ENERGY ASSOCIATED WITH THE SOUL.

Embrace Holy Sophia

What to do and where to go are masculine questions as is the metaphor of a journey to faith. Men want to go off somewhere: desert, mountains, sea or city. But adventurers expend energy outward, instead of drawing inward as "inplorers" and "inventurers." To "know thyself," however, is based on "information" not "out-formation." The notion of a trip to faith applies only as a metaphor due to the turmoil created by self-doubt.

When you realize you are there, the journey is over, even as a metaphor. You can be alienated but never separated from a place that exists within your own mind. There is no divorce from the source and the guru is always you. A fundamental distinction, then, is being there now via awareness. The task is not gender specific even though inwardness culturally is considered feminine. As the offspring of God the Father and Holy Sophia the Mother, men and women both bear a Light.

The roles of men and women in society reflect the psychic split into gender identities. Union means psychological wholeness via integration of masculine and feminine dimensions in the personality. Romantic love is often practiced, however, to replace spiritual communication with the excitement of emotion and sensation. Thus, psychic impediments can block the way to the Holy Grail and the Holy Girl.

Being There Now

Darth Vader knows romantic love can draw men and women toward spiritual union and he attacks both virulently. Without contact with Holy Sophia, physical love may stop short of higher consciousness. Peace knighthood does not require celibacy, or renunciation of pleasure, but men and women typically make sex and marriage incompatible with peace (Chapter 9).

Femininity is also a way of being in the outer world, but the search for the meaning of life encompasses a way of being feminine inwardly. It involves receptivity to spiritual surrender and a vigorous desire to master consciousness. Willingness is the foremost inner act that signals readiness to transition. Consciousness fixed on worldly affairs, however, prevents the passion for Holy Sophia. Mel Gibson's *The Passion of the Christ* (Newmarket Film Group 2004) for example, depicts having faith as intense physical suffering instead of deep joy.

FIVE

MENTOR SEEKING

The *Empire Strikes Back* is the middle act in the *Star Wars* drama and the bleakest period of the rebellion. Accordingly, it is set in the frozen waste world of an ice planet where the alliance has retreated after victory over the imperial army at the end of *A New Hope*. Via teamwork, Han and Luke are now comrades, but Han and Leia are still locked in a caustic romantic rivalry.

On a reconnaissance patrol at the beginning of this episode, Luke is (again) knocked unconscious and dragged by a grisly snow monster to an icy cavern where he is hung upside down on a hook to be slaughtered. We are alerted that something important is about to happen because he was previously knocked out by desert creatures just before enlistment in the crusade of moral knights.

NOVICE & MENTOR

Two True Teachers

The bleak landscape serves as a metaphor for the state of the rebellion at this time. As Luke's mood and the confederate cause plummet, bad weather forecasts the prospects for peace. The resistance to giving up violent old ways persists, even though suffering is only prolonged. More fighting is a setback also because there is absolutely no hope for victory in this direction

Using *psychokinesis*, Luke extracts his light saber jammed in the snow nearby, reminiscent of young King Arthur removing a sword held fast in anvil and stone. As the monster prepares to devour him, Luke severs its shaggy arm and escapes, but lacking the strength to return to the rebel base, collapses in the tundra. To introduce a new way of thinking he apparently needs to be unconscious.

Obi-Wan now appears as a visage, not to reassure Luke about his predicament, but to announce a new rebel strategy — reassignment to training with Master Yoda. Obi-Wan, formerly known as gentle "Ben Kenobi," has retired from active service to disguise his role as Luke's guardian. Only two teachers of truth remain alive to oppose the unrestrained malice of Darth Vader.

The meek permit peace while the strong resist it. People often adopt faith when weakened by accidents, illnesses and near death experiences. Delirious, Luke seems lukewarm about the transfer and not sure he comprehends the message. In the meantime, Han comes to his rescue and reminds him, in good-natured sibling rivalry, "That's two you owe me, junior."

Against the backdrop of galactic warfare, Luke flies boldly and swiftly to his destination, accompanied by his intrepid robot-navigator-aide, Artoo Detoo. In rapid transit, the fighter pilot is wrought with worry. Rooted in self-mistrust, the remote location of the training facility suggests just how unaware Luke is that the civil war is a product of his thinking.

PSYCHOKINESIS: THE ABILITY TO MOVE PHYSICAL OBJECTS WITH THE MIND.

NOVICE & MENTOR

RESISTANCE

Militantly, Luke flies to his training base piloting a fighter spacecraft with a frown that must be relinquished to appreciate mind power and to become a peace knight. He gets to the second level of apprentice, before fearing success, suspending training and retreating to the galactic war for "safety." Fighting with others is a common defense against gaining higher consciousness that covers up fear with anger.

The intra-psychic dimension of the war is highlighted by parallel scenes in which Luke's comrades, Han Solo and Princess Leia, evade Darth Vader's pursuit by hiding in a cave on a flying asteroid that turns out to be, like *Jonah and the Whale*, the interior of a "giant space slug." Caught-up in the sphere of their egos, Han and Leia engage in a competitive chase.

The term "engagement" refers to marriage and to warfare. In Spanish, *casar*, "to marry," is close to *cazar*, "to hunt" — *la caza* is "the hunt" while *la casa* is "the house." Jokes abound that confound the two. Marital and martial may look alike in English, but at least sound different (Chapter 9).

Within the larger war with Darth Vader, Han and Leia become entangled in an awful feud, but once alone, in the belly of the beast, they turn ravenous for one another. The pair eventually overcome their mutual loathing, fall deeply in love and bond with the Force. As the secular sexual couple, however, neither is ever trained or knighted, in contrast to Luke and Yoda, the asexual pair of Jedi Knights in training.

Luke's driving ambition is to be remembered in the annals of time as a great war hero in space. He expects to break from the fighting, be trained quickly, return to the front, defeat the enemy and save rebel civilization. Yet, he doubts that he possesses the capacity to become a Jedi Knight. En route, close-ups reveal the personal struggle he endures. Childishly, he hides, rather than confront his misgivings, adding to his "weakness."

Clones Mimic Thinking

The acceptance of fear separates fledgling from full-fledged peace knights. Eventually you learn to press forward via initial trust in mind power. In soaring away during the transition from outward militancy to inner self-confidence, Luke is "sore afraid." The denial of fear causes the return of guilt as "enemies" who attack like clones mimicking exactly what you think.

Luke worries that he will not find his guide and not accomplish his mission. As a test of character, he fears he may prove corrupt, mentored by the dark side of his mind like his father. His foul self-doubt is reinforced when he is confirmed as the genetic son of Darth Vader. Conceived before, but born after his father's fall, "born in sin" is the reason he engages the clash.

Everyone is 'The One'

The contradiction between Luke's solid plan and his lack of confidence expresses a psychic tug of war. In truth, the only obstacle he has to overcome is his self-doubt, but it is too early in the quest, and he is too young to know, for he would then already be what he seeks to become. To acknowledge your true self can only be imagined to be difficult. Soldier or civilian, anyone can be a peace knight because everyone already is one.

As Luke and Artoo Detoo approach the planet, flight instruments indicate that no civilization lies below — only animal and plant "life-forms." The education Luke is about to undergo is organic. In a hurry to be trained and to win the war, however, he crashes his spacecraft. Wanting to become a new kind of fighter, he rushes headlong into the mission without finding a parking spot.

Symbolically, Luke is swamped by primal guilt and self-doubt at the start. If you are afraid to be who you really are, it is easy to make mistakes, get lost and not to find your guide. Extricating himself, Artoo Detoo falls overboard, but before he drowns, is swallowed by a giant serpent, the appearance of intensified fear at the threshold of change. The underwater danger again suggests that the outer conflict conceals an inner one.

Artoo Detoo is spit out, however, because the worm of the underworld, another form of the devil, seeks to devour the human soul, not the metallic body of the robot. Luke is relieved that he did not slip and fall, and tells his companion, "You're lucky you don't taste very good." Back on *terra firma*, spared consumption by the vile reptile at the genesis of his quest, Luke does not know what to do nor what a mentor looks like.

When you begin to explore, you understand little about the land you enter or the nature of your quest. Shocked and dismayed at first, you perceive only that the new way threatens a customary lifestyle. Fearful, you are not sure you want to grow. Resistance is inherent in any new undertaking and impatience reflects misgivings about your potential. The known may bore us but the unknown terrifies us.

Resistance marks the journey to faith, but in looking for Master Yoda, Luke starts to learn the first lesson — willingness, the desire to develop. He continues to be willing, trusting that he will find his idol, by not allow obstacles — like leaving comrades, flying into the wilderness, crashing his spacecraft, losing his computer overboard and not knowing the way — to deter his pursuit. Will-ingness refers to being a tiny bit open minded about the prospect of meeting your destiny.

Lesson One: Willingness

On account of the urgency of the galactic civil war, Luke already has decided to pursue peace knighthood and, therefore, the prerequisite of willingness is taken for granted in the film. His aspiration is shown first by believing a mentor exists and second, by searching for Yoda. A wisp of will initiates the journey, as he wants to become familiar with the power of his mind.

A Wisp of Will

You must first have a desire to learn. A receptive attitude is appropriate for wisdom heroes who try to let go of coercion in all endeavors. Being "required to volunteer" or "compelled to join," contradict the integrity of mind power that is given unconditionally. In *The Matrix*, Morpheus says to Neo, for example, "I can only show you the door, you're the one that has to walk through it."

Willingness sounds redundant when put into words. To be a wisdom hero you must want to be a wisdom hero. You must want and ask for it. The desire must arise from the consent of your mind as an act of free will. You can join peace knights with a divided mind but not in total opposition. If you hesitate, you make a mistake, but it is never too late.

Willingness initiates the process of change that does not involve sacred covenants, solemn oaths or pledges of allegiance. There are no esoteric secrets to uncover, no karma to repay for past life mistakes, no qualifying examinations to pass, no rites of passage to negotiate, no occult lore to memorize, no advanced fees and fines to pay and no big commitment to make.

You do not face an ordeal of bravery, undertake elaborate rituals, toil long and hard by day and night, acquire the discipline of a disciple, give up worldly pursuits, vow poverty or abandon sensuality. Willingness is not the product of physical ability, intelligence, pri-

WILLINGNESS
- ♦ Your own free will
- ♦ Tiny .01%
- ♦ One time decision
- ♦ One step program
- ♦ Does not require consciousness
- ♦ Consciousness speeds up process
- ♦ Impossible by threat or coercion
- ♦ Effects evidenced empirically later
- ♦ Involves no work

---

vilege, class, race, gender or any physical attribute. Knighthood depends not upon social or genetic breeding.

It is a mistake to try to prove yourself worthy through some test of resilience rather than by simply volunteering. A little willingness means that you can remain uncertain about becoming a peace knight. The fulfillment of your destiny rests solely on an initial decision — "now" is the time and "here" is the place to begin the transition. Willingness is not strenuous or treacherous.

Patience does not endure frustration, tolerate pain and defer gratification. If you think you have learned to wait, but do not like it, you are still impatient. Without pressure, willingness makes you innocent of guilt in your heart long enough to recognize that your assignment as a wisdom knight has begun. Typically, however, fighters want conquests and parades.

So, it takes a real hero to appreciate the anonymity of peace knighthood. Willingness is being open, so that what is within your mind can flower and flourish. If you have to prove anything to anyone, including yourself, you do not believe you deserve to begin. You need to locate peace only once, and with prepaid intuition, an inner academy begins to take over your faculties.

The Force Uses No Force

To be peaceful is to master your mind. It happens when you want it and you need to want it only once. You speed up the process when remembering that you want to learn peace. If you think it takes time, it does, because in the interim you are not willing. You can always change your mind and return to not wanting to acquire rational faith by keeping the desire unconscious.

You cannot halt the transformation once it starts. The initiation works on your behalf to help you to be restored to your original sense of wholeness. Your healthy mind knows when you are ready to risk the leap to faith via the noble hero's quest for wisdom. To begin is only one step and the master plan is out of your hands. The Force uses no force.

You need not strive, but only permit your legacy to be known. Once started, diversions will appear along the way. To say, "Within my limits, I am willing," is not willing because you first establish a barrier. Further, it is self-defeating to exaggerate the objective of faith by distorting it out of range. It is not necessary to cause oceans to rise, cities to fall or to achieve the impact of a meteor.

Head for Peace & Peace Heads for You

Wanting to remain at peace may seem hard, but staying upset and hostile — not maturing mentally — is even harder. Willingness cannot be difficult because it is just an innocent attitude. Thinking he has to become a new type of warrior, while in fact mistaken, awakens Luke's desire. But you may insist that it is beyond your capacity if you wish. (*Me? A peace knight? Nah . . .*).

The difference between willing and becoming is not a fine point — it is the only point. It is the difference between remaining guilty and undeserving versus being guiltless and deserving. The truth is, you must honor the law of faith one time. The intention preempts all previous programming. You usually do not suddenly transform, due to reservations, though theoretically it is possible. When you *head* for peace — peace *heads* for you.

Beyond Willingness

Willingness implies self-trust, not whole-hearted at first, but enough to get started and it breaks the frame of extraverted consciousness. It is "deep" in that it involves insight, in contrast to superficial thinking that tries to impress others with appearances. The false self is never so deeply ingrained, however, that it cannot be overcome by wanting to learn. Forever does the "dark side" control your destiny only until you change your mind and decide to get out.

Within the system, without remembering your right mind and wanting to leave, there is no hope of escape. There is no penalty for remaining in the dark, except the personal hell created by your lack of faith. But if you hesitate, it means you are still attracted by guilt to psychic and physical pain. You can procrastinate after you are willing because inconsistency is a level of commitment — .01% or less initiates the process.

Beyond willingness is dedication, reverence, adoration, vigilance and absolute devotion. This level of commitment is difficult to achieve because it requires strict discipline to counteract a severe sense of guilt that arises from an original decision to leave heaven, enter the dense world, encapsulate in a body and inflate an ego. Attempting "iron will" indicates that you still think it is your power that transforms you and replaces God.

You need not "sheer will" but "mere will." You do not "have to want it hard enough" but "just want it." A platitude says, "Where there is a will, there is a way." In the beginning, it is not necessary to believe the outcome will improve the quality of your life or end the civil war in your mind. Only one level of commitment is required — to be willing to start. Prefer to be a peace knight, rather than not preferring and starting is done.

Because mind power works through you, once you want to be led, the process operates in reverse: a peace knight becomes you. You do not "master the Force" nor does "the Force master you" because it is not a wrestling match or a chess game. It is mere acknowledgement of what is already given. Believing you must discharge all self-doubt prevents you from having the little courage to begin.

A Peace Knight Becomes You

You take the first step and do not know the outcome in advance. You learn the four principles along the way and discover your destiny. The principles are all psychological and involve changes only in disposition and perception. No other action is required and willingness to learn is only an attitude. But under the rule of guilt, you think you are never good enough to please God.

Learning does not depend upon repeated lessons, endless practice, or years of experience. It requires only a fraction of the time, money and energy needed to become a professional artist or performer, for example, and it imparts genuine self-esteem. Like breathing, the aspiration to be mature psychologically is natural. You want peace and will be a peace knight.

Knighthood is neither a grave undertaking nor a matter of total dedication. Seriousness of mind and absolute devotion belong to accomplished peace knights and not to aspirants. Being too serious is also humorous, so you can laugh at your long face laced with misgivings. Tenacious willingness comes after years of perseverance and service. As a precondition, it is a joke. A beginner is not even required to smile.

Maturity is Natural

To expect accomplishment before initiation asks for graduation before matriculation. In learning anything, you make unreasonable demands when you think you must be capable instantly. Perfectionism scares you away from just wanting to learn how to be healthier and happier. You do not have to be perfect — not one percent of the time — faith that knows no bounds is angelic — beyond earthly instruction.

WILLINGNESS NOT

- Dedication without doubt
- Letting go of all restraints
- Believing totally in yourself
- Taking full responsibility
- Having no reservations
- Unwavering determination
- Absolute commitment
- Following through without fear
- Total faith that you will succeed
- Overthrowing all the old taboos
- Realizing your true goals

---

demands when you think you must be capable instantly. Perfectionism scares you away from just wanting to learn how to be healthier and happier. You do not have to be perfect — not one percent of the time — faith that knows no bounds is angelic — beyond earthly instruction.

Join the Force?

Early lessons are learned with little effort, once you are mentally ready to join the Force. Willingness initiates the unfolding of a contingent set of principles that have a domino effect. Given any percent willingness, it cannot be difficult, though you can say you are willing and not mean it. If .01% is a "leap of faith," try .001%, or .0001%. Being 99.99% imperfect gets the peace ball rolling.

100% Imperfect or .001% Perfect?

Other words for willingness are: to want, to invite, to log on, to desire, to accept, to admit, to apply, to elect, to resolve, to declare, purpose, to dare, to awake, to be tempted and to choose. In the lex--icon of the *Old Testament*, willingness is also known as being "right-minded," "righteous" or "having rectitude." ("I have purposed it, I will also do it" *Isaiah* 46:11).

Willingness is not didactic (preachy) or arrogant, both defensive maneuvers that arise out of fear of not having the capacity to succeed by will alone. You do not make yourself a peace knight — it is already done — you only witness your own ascension. A greater power does all the work to transform you once you recognize that you are the king of beings you long to be.

King of Beings

Do not rush lessons or try to be finished, but stick to the simple task of starting willingly. You do not need to be a child prodigy or identified by wondrous signs in infancy. "The journey of a thousand miles begins with the first step," wrote Lao Tzu, wise founder of Taoism. And, the first step can be taken in slow motion. The only decision to make is to start the unfolding process.

Nothing precedes willingness because there is only one level — wanting to learn to have faith. So, just say "Yes," or "Yes, My Master." Becoming a developed person takes only an instant of volition to being loved by God. "Taking the first step is a milestone," a student once declared. Willingness means basic trust in a mentor, inherent in your mind as part of a greater authority.

Laughter not Obedience nor Defiance

If you feel constrained to carry out a duty to become a peace knight, then you inauthentically seek to be what others want, out of an underlying sense of guilt. If you could be forced to develop, psychological power would not exist and control by outer forces would be total. You would not know it, however, just as you do not know now that you have mind power. The unwritten fifth principle of peace knighthood is laughter, not obedience or defiance.

Six

Mentor Fighting

In *The Empire Strikes Back*, Luke sets out to find Yoda, to learn about the Force and to become a Jedi Knight. Yoda is a venerated sage who knows how to teach mortals the doctrinal and practical ways to mind power. Yoda transmits the law of faith to the rebel people through mentoring Luke. But Yoda is not Yoda until Luke is willing.

Luke doubts the law of faith in himself and suspects that Yoda and the Force are fraudulent. Given the celestial connotations of the name "Skywalker," however, he must possess the Force for he is not called "Skyjacker" or "Jaywalker." But he fears his name may be "Luke Vader." By himself, Luke thinks he must halt the behemoth of brutality, or face doomsday of the civilized galaxy.

Returns to Knighthood

Recovering on the bank of the swamp after crash landing, Luke has a premonition. "Something out of a dream," he says, there is "something familiar about this place." He recalls being in this predicament before, but dismisses the notion. He remembers only vaguely that already he has been trained. In this respect, Luke returns to knighthood rather than starting out for the first time.

Luke senses that he is being watched and is surprised to hear a voice behind him. The sequence of the events confirms the correctness of his intuition but his acuity also frightens him. He spins around, blames his fear on a little green *troll* and threatens to blast him away. Luke's desire for wisdom confirms an old truism — a teacher appears when a student is ready to learn.

Wrong & Ugly

Luke is told patiently to put down his weapon for no harm is meant to him. Actually, Yoda has found Luke and asks, "I am wondering, why you are here?" Luke says, as if Yoda is nobody, "I'm looking for someone." "Found someone, you have, I would say, hmmmmm?" Yoda replies. Luke is looking for "a great warrior," revealing a preconception about the appearance of Jedi Knights.

In his cryptic style, the wizened but wise old Yoda declares, "Wars not make one great." Just as Luke anticipates the nature of his training, he expects Yoda to have an image grander than that of the icon of death, Darth Vader, who wears full body armor, flowing black robes and is two meters tall. It is not bigger or stronger, however, because the power of the mind expands from within.

TROLL: FIGURE IN FOLKLORE : DWARF, ELF, GNOME, GENIE, IMP, OGRE, SPRITE.

At first, Yoda does not measure up to Luke's expectations and is regarded as a bumbling pest. The wise part of the self is tiny in the beginning and thought to be wrong and ugly. Jesus was not recognized as the Messiah to deliver Israel from the Roman occupation, and Socrates, in ancient Athens, was reputed to be short, fat, ugly and unkempt. Judge not a mentor by his stature?

Yoda is a hybrid strain of Jedi Knight, a cross between the physique of Kermit the Frog and the genius of Albert Einstein. His height contradicts the notion that the inner being, or the outer, is a giant. Yoda is small, old, lame, carries a cane ("gimer stick") and appears to be strange. The oracle in *The Matrix* lives in a tenement, smokes cigarettes, bakes cookies, speaks plainly and dies. Luke and Neo perceive only what they preconceive.

Small Body Big Mind

A military professional, Luke is prepared to fight enemies with technology. Yoda wants to help Luke be patient and acquire mind power. But like a child, Luke wants to know, "Where's Yoda?" Well, he is standing undisguised right in front of him. The *Gospel of Thomas* says, "You do not recognize the one who is before you and you do not know how to read the moment." Like Simba in *Lion King* (Disney Studios 1994) Luke cannot wait to be king-knight.

Luke does not recognize Yoda as a master because he does not measure up to awesome expectations. Luke believes the power needed to defeat the enemy is overt physical power and this mistake is precisely the reason that the rebel cause is defeated. The strength of the body is puny in contrast to the mighty wisdom of the mind, but this idea seems odd at first, like Yoda and his teachings.

Mental strength comes from the acceptance of physical weakness. The spiritual and material worlds are opposites, and what Luke thinks is strength is weakness, and vice versa — the mind is powerful. For this reason, Yoda instructs Luke standing him on his head. (In a spacecraft damage report to Captain Solo, See-Threepio also conveys the idea of reverse perspective — "To replace the negatively polarized power couplings").

Reverse Perspective

Luke is afraid that if he backs down in the presence of little Yoda, he will appear cowardly and look like Yoda: small, green, ugly and harmless. Yoda is contemptible because Luke estimates him based on his height of twenty-six inches. This was the size of the model of *King Kong* (RKO 1933) in the *eponymous* depression era motion picture. "Judge me by my size [ears] do you," Yoda retorts defensively. Akin to Walt Disney's Mighty Mouse, Luke cannot imagine a pint-sized master.

A Taut Mind Cannot Be Taught

Luke treats Yoda the way Han treats Luke when they first meet, though Luke does not call Yoda "kid" or "junior." Being small in the natural world makes you a big target of hostility from those who fear being little and it expresses concealed contempt for children. A taut mind cannot be taught.

Play Opens the Mind

In pestering Luke with pranks about how he grew so big eating his strange food, Yoda stoops to Luke's level. This means Yoda is flawed like human beings and not a perfect alien entity. Yoda makes fun of Luke, "Aww, can't you get your ship out?" He rummages through his equipment bag until he finds a flashlight. Annoyed, Luke does not realize Yoda wants to shine away his worry about not succeeding in becoming a Jedi Knight.

Playing with Luke, Yoda tries to help him relax and open his mind to a new way of thinking. When Luke is told, "Yoda. You seek Yoda," suddenly, Luke realizes that the creature knows Yoda and can guide him to his hideout. Luke quickly turns compliant, regarding Yoda expediently now as an ally. Insignificant a moment before, Yoda rivets (ribets?) Luke's attention.

Yoda, who is not yet Yoda to Luke, leads the naive young man to his native cabin, there to eat, rest and recover from the distress of relocation and to prepare to encounter Yoda the Great. Restless, Luke cannot settle his mind and asks incessantly how to find Yoda. Luke must calm down and trust, but he thinks he needs immediate training to save the galaxy from ruin.

EPONYMOUS: THE PERSON FOR WHOM SOMETING IS NAMED.

Yoda's goal is not to test Luke to see if he has the "right stuff" as if he were training him for conventional warfare. The question is, will Luke be patient enough to allow the process to unfold — will he permit real power to occupy his thinking? Still, knighthood is Luke's legacy, whether he is patient with inspiration, or impatient with desperation at the start.

True Inner Self

When Luke relaxes just a little, he demonstrates the requisite attitude of willingness. Then he is formally ready to meet Yoda and together to move on to the next principle. Relaxation ushers in patience and allows the prospect of knighthood to enter consciousness. Trans-formation occurs more slowly when willingness is kept unconscious and forgotten.

LESSON TWO: PATIENCE

To guide his destiny in becoming a peace knight, Luke replaces thinking, based on the bodily sensation, with thinking based on introspective wisdom. The love Luke learns to honor arises from the resource of his true self and makes him whole. Because the material world is all Luke remembers having known, the new perspective initially seems incomprehensible.

In the beginning, knowledge appears in an unexpected form, the way the new world showed up as America, instead of India, for European explorers. The inertia of ignorance must be overcome by wanting to learn to have faith. Peace knighthood is not a reward for patience, because it is already given, but you know that it belongs to you through having this attitude.

Stillness & Silence

In stillness and silence you claim the truth of who you are. Your relaxed state of mind allows unconscious knowledge to surface. But Luke is preoccupied with the geographical location of his guide. A racing mind blocks intuitive wisdom. Being patient means you wait with hope while not feeling guilty about "wasting" time.

Luke's training begins by learning that relaxation leads to revelations in thinking. Yoda tells Luke, "Only a calm mind knows the difference between good and evil" (or has a sense of humor, knowing a good from a bad joke). As the son of a natural born pod-racer, perhaps Luke inherited impatience from his father?

To Wait & Hope

As a brazen adolescent Luke says haughtily, "We're wasting our time." Yoda himself now loses patience and blurts out irritably, "I cannot teach him. The boy has no patience." Yoda is agitated. Luke tests Yoda's patience, just as Yoda tests Luke's, as the two learn together. Luke at least shows he can concentrate in a way required later to absorb Principle 4: Mind Power.

To be patient means not to wait in a hurry nor give up while wanting for personal change to take effect. Yoda's reaction is surprising, given that he is the most intelligent creature in the galaxy with 900 plus years of experience in educating novices. An impatient mentor can only teach impatience. Yoda is an imperfect and also perfectly divine.

In Spanish there is a saying, *quien espera desespera* (whoever waits despairs) but the exact opposite is true, revealed in the fact that "to wait" and "to hope" are the same verb: *esperar*. *Yo espero* means both I wait and I hope, that is, to wait patiently is to hope. Similarly, *realizar* is not "to realize," a false cognate, but "to achieve." *Yo creo* means both "I believe" and "I create."

Espero & Creo

Few adults have patience because we grow up *rapido* to gain access to the microwave oven, jet engine, instant network society. At age twelve, you are in a big hurry to be sixteen so you can get a driver's license and date. Then you want to be twenty-one to drink, gamble and stay out all night. Next you want a good job, new boy-girlfriend, fast sports car and to speed to *fiestas* to dance *salsa* and swing.

There is no way to know whether development takes place at longer or shorter intervals, faster for some and slower for others. Patience helps you hold onto hope while awaiting the unexpected. It prevents you from giving up during delays and gets you out of the race to be an ace. You would not be in a big hurry if you did not feel guilty about wasting time and about what you were doing while wasting it.

Out of the Ace Race

After Yoda makes himself known, Luke realizes his training has begun. Exasperated, Yoda announces that Luke's training is over. Yoda tells Obi-Wan's spiritual presence that Luke's attitude is too rigidly fixed. "Much anger in him, like his father." Obviously, there is much anger in Yoda too. "He is too old. Yes, too old to begin the training." Yet, Yoda is much older. In contrast, Artoo Detoo is ageless for his chrome dome spins 360 degrees in either direction.

Luke is just twenty-one, while Yoda is over 900 years old. Yoda thinks Luke craves excitement and implies that he is ready to ship him back to the outer battle, where Luke (and Yoda) are mentally in the moment. Perhaps Yoda needs to review "patience" in the basic training manual. Reportedly, it took four hours to film every two lines of Yoda's dialogue, making the fee for sage exorbitant.

When Luke figures out that the creature is Yoda — THE JEDI MAN — undaunted by his previous blunders and audacity, he begs Yoda to stay and promises to reform. Luke fears expulsion from training, poor grades at the academy, unsupportive letters of recommendation, failure to graduate and the loss of the great civil war. Obi-Wan intercedes, however, to remind Yoda that the two of them were once rash, just like Luke.

Patience is the Shortcut

The fast track to knighthood is what father Anakin sought from Obi-Wan during his training days. Patience is the shortcut to knighthood. Acting humanly irascible, Yoda shakes his head dolefully, but agrees to give Luke another chance. Obi-Wan assures Yoda that Luke will complete his mission. Luke eagerly accepts instruction now and says he is not afraid. But still fallible, Yoda warns with a scrutinous eye, "You will be. You will be."

Forget to Forgive

Yoda's reaction shows that advanced knights can lose their composure and sense of humor. For example, Yoda threatens Luke, "You will be afraid," scolds him for being "too adventurous," yells at him, "You must learn to control" and disparages him by shaking his head. Yoda acts like a drill sergeant. He is not perfect and the remote assignment may be the penalty for his intransigence.

Losing patience while teaching patience may be funny, but by his example, Yoda teaches impatience. Luke is not going to learn to wait, and to trust, entirely from this great master. In being flawed, however, Yoda shows that the capacity to be a peace knight lies within mortal reach. A cranky imp at times, Yoda is less oracle-like and more vulnerable as a little ogre.

Forgive your flaws when you are perturbed, for you forget also that you are divine — and forgive to forget. Holding onto guilt is choosing not to forgive. A peace knight may try to give everything to a higher cause, but this does not mean there are never lapses or regressions. Wings and halos are not standard issue. You are on the path even while lost in the wilderness most of the time.

Forgive to Forget

From experience you believe you have something negative to overcome before you can be willing, but there is really no impediment. Do not focus on wrongs of the past, concentrate on mind power in the present. Though Luke signs up to be a better fighter, his intention is enough. If you think something more is required, you are not yet willing. You need the will of a rookie not a wookie — never too little to begin — and patience comes in time.

Luke longs to inhabit the peace of mind of a higher self whose existence he intuits but does not yet know how to attain. In place of fantasies of conquest by the action hero, willingness starts to fill-in consciousness with the law of faith in the budding wisdom hero. Truth is cognized and then recognized, the second act confirming the first, as tranquility is instilled.

Acknowledge a Mentor?

Mentor Being

You first glimpse emerging knighthood as you react with greater ease to incidents that used to activate your "fight-flight instincts." As you become more tolerant of others, subtle changes show that your thinking is being turned upside-down. Empirically tested faith lifts a contentious, old way of thinking and you feel better in knowing peace belongs to you.

You enter a second stage — apprenticeship — and encounter someone in a new or old relationship, to whom you give advice, based on your new understanding. Self-consciously, you may quote your mentor, but not usually with acknowledgment. Your patience helps this novice turn into an active student of consciousness, who acquires willingness from your acceptance of their awkwardness as a beginner.

Active Student of Consciousness

This collaboration accelerates your movement into apprenticeship and reinforces their initiation. For this reason, during training, two peace knights always work together (the Rule of Two). "The work" is mental though it may appear interactional as if existing between two individuals. The bond is given externally because you believe it is valid only when it confirms your preconceptions.

Rule of Two

The real change takes place in your mind, but it is not recognized in this location by you, or others, because you look the same outwardly, where attention is still fixed. As you acquire patience, following willingness, however, you reinforce development. Your novice will graduate to apprentice when you entertain discipleship, since the two of you move forward in tandem. The reward of teaching is learning (ACIM).

Your Training Case

Your training case is assigned to help you learn what you teach. This might be called the "chain of command" among peace knights, but it is informal and mutual. Thereafter begins the journey to the third and fourth rungs, disciple and master. Now you proceed on your own, as you must come to terms with the Rule of One (i.e., the Law of Faith). Or, you can hang out in the kingdom of appearances as an apprentice for the rest of your days if you wish.

Novice to apprentice is accomplished rather quickly with little effort. But the journey to faith beyond the elementary two levels arouses great resistance. Your imagination will conjure up violent encounters, for example, with a sordid pair of Sith Knights, master and apprentice in training, who want to stop your spiritual growth. By provoking anger to cover fear about aging and dying without the love of God, the underlying guilt attracts you to the imaginary "dark side."

Rule of One

This turns into a major battle with fear and self-doubt. From the ego there is dread also about punishment from God for not previously having had faith. At this point, people unite in groups to establish common enemies as a shield from the anticipated retaliation. The immediate payoff is sharing a goal and bonding with others as an aroused public. The cost is the alienation from God that divides the self into allies and foes and creates warfare.

Ironically, the decision to grow spiritually stimulates the fear of God. If you forgive your self-sabotage (in believing the deity is punitive) and stay aware that you confront but an illusory part of your own split mind, progress will follow. When you lapse in consciousness, however, you will feel assailed by pair of terrorists and eventually by the whole phantom army of enemies. We persist perennially believing that we are misled, rather than guided, by rational faith.

Since the trip becomes arduous, few begin disciple and master training. Humanity stays disturbed by wanting to live forever physically instead of learning to live faithfully. Health, purpose, creativity, fun, joy and dying in peace follow. Not understanding his own disloyalty, Saint Paul suffered the dilemma, saying, "For the good that I would I do not: but the evil which I would not, that I do." (Romans 7:19). The burden of guilt in being mortal is almost too heavy for humans to bear.

Trying to convince yourself that you are worthy of the love of God exaggerates the task and is hateful to you. To think that you decide whether God loves your or not is arrogant. You are not in charge of God's love. Just because your mind is split, does not mean God is divided about you. No matter what you think and do in life, you are absolutely loved and this never changes. Think one iota that this is true — you end your own — and the world's misery.

Hidden Guilt → Alienation from God → Split Mind → Allies & Foes → Warfare

From: robertaduran@msn.com
To: jsnodgr@calstatela.edu
Subject: no more fighting
Sent: Sat, Sep 11, 2004

No Mas!

Yodo teaches Lupe that evil does not exist. Lupe is stubborn believing for a lifetime that she lives in a world outside her mind. Lupe fights what she is being taught, but not to challenge Yodo. Thinking evil exists, you react according to this misconception.

Through loving Yodo as a mentor, Lupe ends the battle, and Yodo reciprocates. In *The Matrix*, Nea struggles for three full-length films and in *Star Wars*, Lupe endures six feature films before she understands. To reverse perspectives and to perceive the real world as an illusion takes time.

Seven

Lesson Three: Phantom Enemy

The third lesson continues Luke's introduction to the mystery of the Force. Yoda rides around the planet strapped to Luke's back like his conscience. Luke thinks that he is preparing to study the art of warfare and that he must get in physical, instead of mental, shape. He runs, jumps and swings because motor skills must be practiced constantly to be effective.

As the two rest together after exploring the terrain, Yoda tells Luke, "A Jedi's strength flows from the Force. But beware of the dark side. Anger . . . fear . . . aggression. The dark side of the Force are they . . . If once you start down the dark path forever will it dominate your destiny." As the message sinks in, Luke is worried because he "failed" patience and thinks he is about to be tested again.

Fear of Physical Weakness

Luke suddenly feels a chill of fear — a premonition about being alone and vulnerable in a dangerous place. Still caught-up in a competitive, old way of thinking, based on feelings of strength and weakness in his body, he is threatened by the sensation and enters the jungle to conquer the peril via confrontation. He thus repudiates Yoda's principle of patience to penetrate the "dark side."

Like a magnet, physical weakness draws you to the "dark side." In following bodily impulses, he boldly disregards the precept of mind power, fearful of Yoda, the jungle and the Force. Luke transfers an insecure way of thinking onto the environment and then believes safety lies in might and arms. Yoda tells him that where he is going, "Your weapons . . . you will not need them." Mental strength needs no reassurance by attack or defense.

Whether you fight or join the "dark side," you lend it credibility whenever you enter its domain and engage on its terms. Being mad about war means fright and fight govern your mind — the war against war is still war. To not fear dying is impossible as long as you believe fighting for anything, including life itself, is worthwhile. "Resist not evil," means not to join, but also not to oppose it, because either way makes the terror seem real.

War Against War Still War

The *Qur'án* (*Koran*) says, "to repel evil with good." The "dark side" has power only when you give it credence. Whether you win or lose a battle, Darth Vader always wins the war because your mind is limited to the hostile boundaries he defines. You cannot defeat someone whom you allow: to name the contest, the slope of the playing field, the terms of engagement, the definition of scoring and the meaning of victory.

Darth Vader is the champion of pathos and chaos that result from self-attacks concerning the physical weaknesses of aging and dying without faith. A war against biology is irrational because the life of human beings is terminal. Fighting makes the "devil" appear stronger, just as the Emperor magnifies the dread of Darth Vader. Agent Smith in *The Matrix* trilogy cannot be defeated because he replicates by fighting him. "Evil" is a double-edged sword: first you think it exists and then condemnation reinforces it.

Whether small or large, evil is an illusion. But Luke repudiates Yoda's inward principle and experiences yet another humiliating loss of power. "Fighting for peace" perpetuates conflict because it always provokes reprisals that appear to trap you in the "dark side." The terms of repulsion between aggressors are mutual and keep vengeance activated. No threat, or use of force, makes peace possible.

To "surrender" does not mean to admit defeat, nor to fake another delay in the fighting, but to accept a new style of thinking. "We are going to have peace even if we have to fight for it," said World War II General Douglas Macarthur. In a contest of egos, however, peace never was his intention. The war against war begins in your mind and ends, according to insight, wherever you may go in the world.

In reacting to Yoda as if there were no option, Luke reveals his ongoing ambition to attain power in a misalliance with the empire. That he thinks he knows how to defeat the demon man means he is in "danger," for he has no guide and therefore, reason to be afraid. Yoda does not order Luke to enter the jungle; it is his obstinate decision. Luke ignores Yoda, rather than his fear, attracted to aggression to repudiate his guilt over feeling physically weak.

Without a guide, hardly anyone discovers or adopts the law of faith in God. Cooperative learning is the opposite of basic military training, done anonymously, under rigid regulations, in large units, relying on intimidation and punishment for failure. Any meaningful communication between instructor and soldier contradicts the objectives of death and destruction. Military personnel trained in meditation to improve concentration lose the will to fight.

War Parties Are No Fun

God is heard through your amazing mind, not your big ears that are attached to the helmet of your hard head. Whether a tree falls in a forest, or grows in Brooklyn, is irrelevant compared to whether you allow your mind to attune to its awesome power. War parties are costly and no fun. The only losses involved in spiritual growth are the cost of arms, battle fatigue and the agony of defeat.

Believing he faces a test of courage, Luke buckles on his weapons belt anyway. He does not realize that Yoda orchestrates the lesson as he calmly sits there toying a "gimer stick." Luke decides to enter a cave in the jungle that represents his unconscious mind. Yoda lets him think that his way is better, before introducing the power of his mind that is hidden "underground."

> *In addition to using the gimer stick to walk and as a 'weapon' against Artoo, Yoda carries the stick to . . . well . . . chew on it. According to Slavicsek's "Guide to the Star Wars Universe," 'The gimer plant produces a succulent juice that gathers in sacs on the bark. The sticks can be chewed for their flavor and to quench thirst. Yoda . . . was fond of chewing gimer sticks.'" Yoda is not impervious to all external influences.* (Anita Backory).

Hard-Headed Helmet

In defiance, Luke maintains the power struggle with Yoda and the Force, preventing communication with his trainer, keeping him at a distance with anger. Luke defends, not against injury, but against gaining consciousness. He wants to deploy weapons instead of employ conceptions, as the fury of a weak body is aroused as a defense against the power of the mind. He believes he must kill his natural father, making the horror and terror seem real.

CHICANERY

Yoda toys with his "gimer stick" as part of a disguise to appear feeble and innocuous. The cane serves many purposes: walking, chewing, warding off R2-D2 and projecting holographic lessons about Jedi Knighthood. As a pointer, it helps keep Yoda himself on the point of faith in the Force.

Luke thinks Jedi Knights are specially trained devil-killing monks. He takes his weapons because he believes there is an enemy and an armed search will find a deadly one. Like dreams, reality seems vivid while you are not conscious. Luke wants revenge — to eliminate his father. He has to be taught not to rage and rampage. The Emperor, who killed his foster parents and Obi Wan, who told him Darth Vader killed his father, have sent Luke down this path.

Furious Weak Body

In the third lesson, as in Plato's classic *Allegory of the Cave*, Luke enters his deeper mind, depicted as descent underground. Creepy snakes, lizards and rats at the portal portend the danger he thinks he will encounter in this primitive place, but he is destined to find gentle mind power. The spiritual self also resides beneath the surface in "Zion" in *The Matrix* trilogy.

Suddenly, a holographic Darth Vader appears to Luke's immediate left. The virtual image suggests a phantom figure arising as a projection from the imaginative side of Luke's right brain. Luke draws his laser sword first and matching blow for blow, decapitates the icon of evil with the first swipe. So easily is he done in, Luke must be tricked, for you cannot overpower "the devil" when he exists nowhere outside your thinking.

or Gentle Mind Power?

Darth Vader's signature black helmet falls to the ground and after Yoda's magical huff and puff, the sight of his own face inside the helmet shocks Luke. His wide-open eyes stare back in disbelief.

HELMET HEADED

Discovering his own face within the helmet of a beheaded Darth Vader, Luke Skywalker thinks that Yoda teaches him, "I am my own worst enemy." But the lesson is about the helmet, about his hardheadedness in believing enemies exist at all. As long as Luke stays obstinate and militant, he has no alternative to being a warrior at war with evil in the world.

No Enemy Anywhere

This is no faceless storm trooper from an alien realm. Luke sees himself and must think, "I have met the enemy and he is me." Mary Henderson (1997) wrote, "Darth Vader is not an external evil presence but the shadow side of Luke himself."

In the third lesson, the enemies you think you see outwardly are actually projected aspects of your own personality. Luke must begin to trust that opponents in his mind are also not real. The enemy is not you, nor your evil twin-clone, for there is no enemy anywhere. Further, Luke must trust the truth that Yoda is a reliable mentor who differentiates fabrications from creations.

No Worst Enemy

When Luke decapitates Darth Vader and discovers his own startled face within the fallen helmet, Yoda says nothing, trusting the experience to convey the message. But most cadets misunderstand the lesson to mean "the enemy is within me." This is a mistake that bars the way to knighthood in believing guilt is real. The issue is insistence on using the anti-Force of physical might to repudiate bodily weakness instead of surrendering to mind power.

Being beheaded suggests getting rid of guilt the way Darth Vader tosses out the Evil Emperor in the finale. Luke was taught to feel guilty as a child (Chapter 10) and he re-engages his acquired enemy-self wherever he turns as an adult, because he encounters his projection as "reality." If he deposes militancy (helmet-headedness) he ascends to a new level of understanding. Thus, "meeting the enemy in me," or in anyone, is refuted.

Believing like his father that the enemy is real, Luke at first takes a martial stance. But the truth is — the enemy does not exist — no Darth Vader in reality and no evil in Luke Skywalker. Seeing no difference, a student once declared, "I believe in Satan as much as I believe in Jesus Christ!" Without a choice, outer control looks total and you do not know it. But with mind power, you can decide to stand in the dark or in the Light.

God is one almighty being, indivisible into good and bad, for true power knows neither opposite nor scope. Oneness means God is non-splitable into dark and light forces except during hypothetical separations from Her. As one absolute being of all within all, no finite power can rival His infinite power, except among those who imagine death of the body to be the end of life. Death is a phantom enemy and all foes are false (faux foe).

"Evil" becomes a category of fantasy and your perception of self and others is transformed. But Luke is helmet-headed, predisposed to see an opponent who is not there, to keep the ego aroused in the body and to defy the Force. Shielded by a helmet, Luke cannot hear this truth. The helmet traps Luke (and Anakin) in circular reasoning that justifies being furious over expulsion from heaven (and the Order of Jedi Knights).

If coercion is used to teach an alternative point of view, being "helmet-headed" in itself, then wisdom knighthood is ignored. Believing there is no enemy includes mentees who contentiously cite horror stories from the media as proof that mentors are mistaken about the non-existence of "evil in reality." Assumptions go unexamined as long as you think you already know the whole truth. As we project, so shall we perceive.

People project their own "evil" and perceive in others what they believe to be true in themselves. You will see no conflict with another person or group, however, without self-conflict. Your self-concept is behind the enemy you conjure up before you. We blame others for being who we think we are, just as they blame us for being who they think they are. Under the rule of guilt, the higher self appears to be trapped by hostile forces.

Are You an Indivisable?

Retreat From Peace

Mixed up about the nature of power, Luke breaks training and defects to the "dark side." He confuses Yoda with Darth Vader and thinks that both threaten to take away his meager personal might. The thought of a trick is the trick, but he cannot be deceived if he trusts his mind. Luke does not realize that he perpetuates fighting to re-press knowledge and block higher consciousness.

The foremost mind-trick of the "dark side" is to lurk in the unconscious and derive power from thinking that you and Darth Vader evolved from the same stock. Hidden guilt reappears outwardly in the ever-shifting shape of wrongdoers. But in the light of being right-minded, these characters are rendered hapless and helpless. Dracula withers in the daylight, Mr. Hyde is exposed in public and an adolescent boy with a light saber redeems "the devil."

Muscle Never Wins

Your guilt reappears as others guilt when you do not remember that your mind projects reality (perception = projection). Unacknowledged feelings of shame always show up as the malicious misconduct of opponents. Your hidden "taints and blemishes" draw you to confront the "dark side" that appears to be imposed externally. Without the root of concealed self-attack, however, there are no enemies anywhere.

Every time you release preoccupation with the physical, what disappears is not power but terror — for your mind now trusts itself rather than mistrusts the actions of others. Muscle never wins. There is no trap to avoid, nor action to execute, unless you think you are bound to a body in the world like *Prometheus* to a rock. Wary students, however, insist that Yoda tricks Luke to enter the jungle and to confront a real death monger.

War Projects Self-Attack

Luke did not construct his own light saber as was the custom. It was a gift from Obi-Wan and belonged to Luke's father when he was Anakin Skywalker. This means the power of wisdom is handed down personally and inter-generationally. Luke goes beyond good and evil during the climax, fabricating a new light saber that represents his new consciousness, reinforcing the line of wisdom knights.

In Spanish, *saber* is "to know." Having a "light saber" suggests knowing the Light, though this point gets blunted in the technical literature on *Star Wars* where it refers to a one meter long weapon of destruction that hums and glows with the enormous energy radiated by crystal jewels in its handle. In "reality," however, light sabers are aluminum tubes painted fluorescent colors and wrapped in plastic to contain fragmentation.

The reclusive Yoda watches the G.I.-Jedi depart, knowing he will return one day because he already is headed for destiny. Luke needs more defeats in outer skirmishes since he believes that he can be destroyed by the perils "out there." The "dark side" exists only in the imagination, however, and you can choose to be at war or at peace, ruptured or enraptured, wherever you go in the universe.

You can retreat to warfare, convinced power resides in the brawny body and dense matter. You can expel the teacher and march out of the classroom. But never are you trapped, because the answer is contained in your right mind, to wield as you like, whenever you are ready to learn. "Some trust in chariots and some in horses: but we will remember the name of the Lord our God" (*Psalms* 20:7).

PROMETHEUS: A TITAN IN GREEK MYTHOLOGY WHO RULED THE EARTH UNTIL DEFEATED BY THE GODS OF OLYMPUS. HE STOLE FIRE AND THE ARTS FROM HEAVEN TO GIVE TO HUMANITY AND WAS PUNISHED BY ZEUS BY BEING CHAINED TO A MOUNTAINSIDE WHERE HE WAS ATTACKED BY A VULTURE FOR ETERNITY. FREED BY HERCULES, KNOWN FOR STRENGTH AND COURAGE.

Light Saber Wisdom

Love and beauty are invisible as long as you reject sanity and serenity. Believing that guilt is real is just a mistake and a kind of bad habit to break. Fighting begets fighting because, disguised as an enemy-agent, you are always at war with yourself and always losing. Staying fearful arouses attack as a defense and reproduces unconscious guilt that demands the punishment of others who are thought to deserve it because they are wrong.

Trying to stamp out "evil" causes it to rise. Relax and entertain the idea that physical location means nothing and mental attitude means everything in life and death. Where you are in your mind is always where you are, for "reality" is entirely a mental construction and never a place beyond your thinking. Purgatory and hell are states of mind "on earth," along with peace and joy.

MIND POWER: LESSON FOUR

Luke stands on his hands as instructed and attempts to levitate two stones. This act of upside-down juggling may appear odd to the uninitiated. Yoda asks Luke to assume this posture because it graphically depicts the nature of the task and puts it right conceptually. Not knowing that power is mental, you think you are the victim of natural and social forces, but actually it is the reverse.

Sanity & Serenity

The script says Yoda teaches Luke to lift one rock to touch another in the air, and at first it looks like he is getting the hang of it. Then suddenly, Artoo Detoo beeps and whistles frantically, because at that moment, the spaceship sinks deeper into the mire. Luke's fear of losing control and becoming visibly helpless are synchronized in his inability to raise the spaceship.

To trainees, power exists in the universe. To defy gravity and operate as a knight in the open light of day seems dangerous. Mind power puts Luke at risk of losing residual natural power, i.e., to fight and to flee, which the spacecraft represents. Locked into the domain of physical control, Luke does not grasp an inward focus. But consciousness exercises mind power and lets the body rest.

Rational consciousness separates cause and effect and reverses the order (ACIM). Two rocks touching suggest a choice of inner versus outer concentration, but Luke displaces his mind outward and decides to deny that he has an option. He substitutes power in reality for spirit in the mind and protracts the covert mind war with God.

Física
=
Físico

Scientists claim that *ideas* are synthesized in the brain, but have *no idea* where and are not dissuaded by the lack of evidence. The synapse to God, not neurons in the brain, fires the mind. Physics investigates only the effects of isolated thinking by body-egos without realizing that "reality" originates in the split mind. But physics makes reality finite only in theory.

The world is experienced only through the mind, so "reality" derives from the projected self-concept of alienated individuals. Human beings are souls in material exile in need of spiritual repatriation. Wisdom is intuitive but unknown while thinking remains disconnected from God's love. Like earth-centered science, people construct an ego-centered universe.

Ego
Centered
Universe

The gap created by the departure from Heaven is the building block of the universe. "Reality" is an outer effect of phenomenal thinking. For example, in Spanish, *física* is the science of physics but *físico* is vanity. *Real* also means "royal," suggesting that reality is imperial, not empirical. The Dutch graphic artist M. C. Escher, fascinated with drawing shiny spheres that distorted the reflection of the viewer, claimed, "Man's ego is the center of the universe."

Wisdom
is
Intuitive

An egotist wants someone to watch his or her act because a looking-glass self is very fragile. Only a creature of *Artificial Intelligence* (Warner 2001) wants a big ego like human beings. As a scientist, Galileo, confronted the church, but did not realize that a centrifugal force called "gravity" by Newton, fixed us to the surface. Galileo and Newton both knew, however, that spinning makes you dizzy.

The ego breaks the first commandment, "Thou shalt have no other Gods before me," including thyself. While there may be a soul to physics, there is no physics to the soul. Luke tells Yoda that moving stones in the air is different than raising a spaceship, but Yoda insists, "Only different in your mind." Luke does not believe that mass and density are illusions of energy and that the mind is not. So, Luke concentrates on the size of the outer object.

"Breathe," "relax," "focus" are exercises to trust that no separation exists and no existence separates us from God. Your mind is your greatest muscle and not restricted to the brain. It has no height, weight or size because it is linked to an immense power that is undectable to the senses. Mind mutates matter in the same way that fire consumes wood, daylight overtakes darkness, knowledge surpasses ignorance and wakefulness replaces dream states.

You must be willing to see beyond body states to know that both body and soul exist in your mind. Willingness makes you aware of what formerly slipped right by your awareness. Knowledge shows up when your mind opens up. But at first, it will seem like "reality" arises from the outside. Perception derives from believing that your projections are real. Both science and science fiction rely on the same assumption that reality is separate from the observer.

Doubting mental science, Luke says, "I'll give it a try." In perhaps the single most famous line from the film series, Yoda responds tersely, "No! Try not. Do. Or do not. There is no try." Obediently, Luke points his right hand toward the spacecraft and focuses. He dislodges it, but becomes fearful of his effect that confirms mind power. He shifts attention outward to protect himself and loses concentration. It sinks and he gives up complaining, "It's too big."

Thinking Yoda demands the impossible — mind over matter — Luke tries Yoda-Vision only briefly and then powers down. To dem-

DISCIPLE & MASTER

REVERSE PERSPECTIVE

Yoda instructs Luke standing him on his head because lessons reverse worldly intelligence that power is physical. Touching two stones during meditation suggests first contact with mind power, once the principles of willingness and patience are learned. Luke is frightened in making the connection. Justified by the entrapment of his comrades, he quits training midway to return to galactic warfare, ostensibly on a rescue mission, but actually to avoid advanced training. He fears the loss of his meager physical might and reproductive power if he becomes a master peace knight.

---

onstrate mind power, Yoda retrieves the sunken spaceship from the murky waters. The incredulous, Luke says, "I don't believe it" and the wise Yoda replies, "That's why you fail." Luke need not try harder nor practice longer — he must simply trust God in his mind to do the heavy (and Light) work.

Physics conceptualizes a material world because spirit is repressed and attention is extruded. "Reality exists because you think outside your mind," a student once declared in an essay. When you feel that something is missing personally, you will find treachery in natural and social forces. Since what is missing is mental, but its fulfillment is regarded as physical, acquisition only arouses a deeper sense of deprivation. Life crises, however, are kept silent in shame.

Taking action asks your body to make up for something missing psychologically and since this is not possible, you act irrationally. You have to do nothing but to trust in higher consciousness. *In God We Trust* is the coin of an inner realm. There is nothing you cannot do, physically or mentally, once you master life with mental discipline. The search for extraterrestrial and domestic intelligence must start with an inward focus.

Looking for signs of life on Mars means wisdom is obscure here on earth. You see only what you preconceive and your formidable mind creates whatever you intend. Peace knights try to stay aware and practice, but are still learning to forgive and love. Luke tell his himself the task is too difficult because the spacecraft is too big. But he only needs to *remind* himself that his mind is powerful and then the size of the ship matters not at all.

If you think evil exists, it creates evidence in the form of "enemies" who appear to attack you as clones of the separated self. Disregarding the mind, traditional Christians think you are saved only if you act sinless. But grace is given regardless of awareness or compliance. In being eternally loved, age-old enemies, including non-Christians, just fade away. Then moving stones or mountains is trivial in contrast to the miracles you can perform with your mind muscle.

Luke wants to control objects to become a legendary warrior. His ambition contradicts his potential, however, as he wants the new ability for the old purpose of egotistical glory and conquest — the essence of the "dark side." He has not changed perspectives and cannot yet see that true power comes from controlling inner attention and is granted through will power that leads to mind power.

Rational consciousness is based on the forgotten decision to exclude God and instead to see yourself in the world of forms. If you think your mind is in your brain, then your identity is based on being a physical body in the material world. We think we are a body because it is what we perceive, but we perceive we are a body because it is what we think. The illusion is meaningless, however, and neither hard heads, nor hard bodies, stand between heaven and earth.

OXYMORON: CONCEPT WITH CONTRADICTORY TERMS.

You are not expected to not fight God, but only to not conceal it in your mind. Through consciousness, everyone is totally loved, but under denial, God is condemned in a covert mind war. Attentiveness is the natural prayer of the soul," wrote Nicolas Malebranche, a French Roman Catholic priest and philosopher (1638-1715). Luke wants power to pursue fighting and reveals that he still thinks like a little boy who envies bigger boys and grown men. The notion of "peace fighter" is an *oxymoron*.

As you learn that conflict resolution is mindful, previous mis-perception is corrected. Luke believes with his senses that power is external while Yoda knows with his mind that it is internal. Because the task is mental, the goal is to invert your point of view, causing the size of an object to be irrelevant. Apprentices and societies usually delay training at the threshold of wisdom by taking another tour of duty through war zones.

During advanced training you maintain a low profile and learn to accept the love of God. A choice between two illusions, i.e., two rocks, is no choice at all, but two rocks touching means first contact — as conscious and unconscious knowledge of the Force meet. Luke must open his mind to an inner power in order to dissolve hate and restore peace that validates the fourth principle. He can perpetuate the ancient enmity of enemies or option for the united sanity of saints.

EIGHT

TRAPPED AND DEFEATED

By searching for Yoda, Luke shows willingness to develop his mind and gain wisdom. At first he lacks confidence, but as he is mentored, he becomes a patient student. Seeing his own reflection in the helmet of Darth Vader helps him realize that conflict with others is projected self-conflict instead of actual attacks. As a sign of understanding, he levitates two rocks, but lacking trust, drops the project and flees training.

Frightened by the prospect of mind power, Luke decides he must return to fighting for protection. At the gateway to adopting Principle 4, he foresees his friends being captured far away. They represent the parts of his mind that are trapped if he quits, but liberated if he stays in school. To find an enemy, Luke turns fear into anger and escapes to battle. He is no help rescuing his friends in this episode and should have stayed to graduate.

Projection of Guilt

Luke resists spiritual mind power. because it is awesom. He fears he will lose control over life if he gives up physical body power. Lesson four, therefore, is regarded as a trap set by Darth Vader who imprisons and tortures his pals. Guilt underscores his worries about failing and being defeated. Pursuing warfare, anger conceals self-hate and projects guilt demanding others be punished as "enemies."

Luke decides he must confront the mega-terrorist. So, he bails out of training, resumes being a fighter pilot and flies away to perpetuate warfare. To Darth Vader, the captured sundry crew serves as bait to trap Luke. But Luke also fears that romantic aspects of life (Han and Leia) will be sacrificed if he is dubbed "peace knight" (Chapter 9).

Yoda tells Luke "the future is difficult to foresee," but the truth is, his friends will remain caught until Luke wants to transcend inner discord and acquires peace consciousness. Understanding Principles 1 and 2, Luke is halfway to knighthood. Willingness and patience come easily, but phantom enemy and mind power are difficult. The wisdom of faith takes years of struggle and often remains incomplete even among the elderly.

Wisdom of Faith

Luke departs to face Darth Vader for the second time, but immediately confronts the fact that his physical power is rudimentary. The father reminds the son, as if the devil were his higher self, that without consciousness, "Your destiny lies with me, Skywalker." Luke also finds out that Obi-Wan lied to him and that Darth Vader is his natural father. "Not true. That is impossible. No! No!" cries Luke.

Horrified, Luke learns that he must do mortal combat with a sworn enemy and possibly murder his own progenitor. This lends a macabre new twist to the idea of being part of the father's bloodline. As guilt escalates, the revelation that Luke and Satan are kinsmen raises the specter of patricide. Thinking he is genetically linked to the devil crushes Luke's confidence.

Darth Vader promptly amputates his son's right hand and sends into oblivion what Slavicsek called "his father's heirloom light saber." The right-hand symbolizes free will and believing he was "born in sin," saps Luke's energy to fight well and win. Cool, unhanded Luke fights hard, but his adversary has the psychological edge. The son of Satan is damned. Alas, Luke is "luckless."

Right Hand = Free Will

The severity of the trauma is suggested by both losses: hand and saber. During this crucial showdown with Father Vader, Uncle Owen's and Obi-Wan's depiction of his lineage contribute to his enfeeblement. "Luke refuses to join his father and says he would rather die," explained Matthew C. Mohs. Luke drops into the central abyss, lands in the rigging on the underside of the city and clings upside-down to a cross-shaped antenna.

Here in the depths of despair, Luke remembers Yoda's teaching about reverse perspective (mind power) and calls out to Ben. Contradicting gender roles, the new pilot of the *Millennium Falcon* has learned that she too is gifted. Telepathically hearing her brother's plea, Leia flies to retrieve him. He sails away with his sister and her co-conspirators, all of whom have escaped the wrath of the dark lord, except Leia's dear companion, Han Solo.

Densely baptized, Solo is frozen solid and turned over to a bounty hunter for transport to the custody of a wormy mobster. One gets the fat reward; another gets revenge. The mad man of evil rules the realm. Just as Luke feels handless, Han feels powerless at the hands of Luke's malicious parent. By the conclusion of the middle segment, the rebel resistance is scattered, wounded and demoralized. Luke has lost his right hand, light saber, best buddy and joined the satanic gene pool.

Hand & Saber

Denial of Mind Power

To the midpoint of *Return of the Jedi*, frightened by the prospect of mind power, Luke does not become a master wisdom hero. He gives up training believing he will lose his physical ability to combat real enemies — the only power he thinks he retains. He also fears losing the capacity to procreate, expressed subtly in the cold damper put on the hot affair between Han and Leia (Chapter 9).

Like his father, Luke is too impatient and too fearful to face his inner demons — to learn that reality is an illusion and that the Force is not. He remains undisciplined because he does not enter inner space and secure mind power as an astronaut of the soul. He does not change his basic assumption, depart the "dark side," grasp the dimension of pure light within his consciousness.

As a military man, Luke ultimately sees everything in terms of rational thinking based on the irrational denial of mind power. Trained to kill, he is terrified to trust a self that does not vanquish foes. Preoccupied with the literal ways of might, Luke has no vision of the wisdom he prepossesses. Yet, he needs only to put his weapons aside and find peace within for a new age to begin.

Faith Wrapped in Outrage

Luke's resistance resembles our own as we skirmish continuously with those we love and hate. Via guilt, the "bad" son and daughter side of ourselves is attracted to conflict with others. Fighting keeps wisdom insulated in outrage. "The meek shall inherit the earth," for they know not how to fight. We can change our likeness, our "Lukeness," when we decide to ride with the peace knights.

Resumption of Training

In *Return of the Jedi*, all the knights, robots and citizens of deep space reappear. *Episode VI* resumes on Luke's home planet where the fostered child first began his adventures in *A New Hope*. But now he is taken across the barren wastes to witness the obscene lifestyle of the lord of the "spice" trade, the traffiker in illicit drugs in the galaxy.

The renegade Captain Solo is petrified in painful contortions and hung on the wall like a work of modern art. He serves as a grotesque reminder of the punishment for loving Leia and having faith in the Force. A roving messenger, Artoo Detoo, shows up at the dive with a hologram from Luke. To avoid an "unpleasant confrontation," the gangster is advised to release the captive and offered the two robot in exchange.

As Formidable as his Bulk

Apparently, Luke thinks he has to sacrifice both computers to rescue Han and to redeem the ultra hedonist. The conversion of the obese thug of greed to higher consciousness appears to be as formidable as his bulk. Luke follows-up the message by a live appearance and refers to himself a "Jedi Knight." An advisor informs the crime lord, "He's no Jedi." The offer is declined and the loyal robots are relieved.

Disguised as a male bounty hunter, Leia thaws Han with the heat of her steadfast love and rescues him for the first time. When he hears that Luke calls himself a "Jedi Knight," fully humiliated himself, he claims Luke suffers "delusions of grandeur." Luke is imprisoned and Leia, in scanty attire, is manacled by the neck, like a concubine, to the altar of the vice lord. The siblings are trapped, the male shut away in a dungeon and the female exposed on a throne.

The whole contingent of rebel convicts is then transported to the center of an expansive desert to be fed to a gnawing orifice that lives beneath the sand. The voracious cavity represents the isolation of the self via the retention of grudges and hungering for revenge. In the Special Edition, the pit of greed acquired a head and tentacles, but its digestion remained torturously slow punishment for pursuing spiritual awareness.

is the Hunger for Revenge

Out of his innards, Artoo Detoo delivers to Master Luke an improved light saber and the massacre is averted. In the ensuing melee, the hoodlums are all killed off or routed — consumed by the backfire of their own anal plot. Leia single-handedly strangles the slime lord to death with the chain that enslaved her. She fights savagely as an avenging victim who turns on her captor.

Now for the first time, Luke saves Han and begins to repay his debt in the tally of rescues. As soon as his friends are released, Luke is free again to pursue becoming the prince of peace under the tutelage of the frog sage. "The revelation of his lineage, the loss of his hand and his failure to save his friend Han Solo from solidification, demonstrate the need for him to be stronger in the Force," wrote Matthew C. Mohs.

Because Luke evolves as a wisdom knight, Emperor Palpatine and Darth Vader foresee the renewed threat to their regime and team up to drag him back to the "dark side." Given that Luke has ascended to level two, apprentice, it will now take both "evil" characters to stop him. Luke's decision to return to training and his impending promotion to disciple, are the real reasons a master and apprentice from the "dark side" must work together — and even then it is futile.

Luke and Leia believe crimes by their father against humanity must be righted by revenge. But Luke finds Master Yoda on his deathbed. Yoda reminds Luke that he knows what to do and Luke replies, "Then I am a Jedi." But Yoda contradicts him saying he must confront Darth Vader another time. "Then, only then, will a Jedi you be. Unfortunate that you rushed to face him . . . that incomplete was your training. That not ready for the burden were you."

Among fans, Luke is reputed to be Yoda's best pupil and his flight from training is forgotten in nostalgia. Driven by guilt as usual, Luke's mind is still locked into the temporal-territorial plane as he assumes Yoda means another light saber duel with his arch nemesis. A mentor must repeat lessons since trainees continue to miss the point that the quest involves coming to terms with the father of the mind, not the body.

Guilt Driven as Usual

Luke confronts Yoda with the question, "Master Yoda, is Darth Vader my father?" Like Uncle Owen, Yoda turns away, evading an answer, saying he needs to rest. Though all ears, Yoda is not listening. The burden of truth about Luke's inheritance of evil is apparently too heavy even for Yoda the Great to bear. He reminds Luke once again, however, that fighting is folly. "Once you start down the dark path, forever will it dominate your destiny."

Yoda's barely audible last words are a clue that Luke is not alone, "There is . . . another . . . Sky . . . walker" (his sister). At this point, Luke witnesses Yoda's demise after a biblical lifespan, according to an unofficial count, of exactly 973 years. This is longer than Methuselah who lived to age 969 (*Genesis* 5:21). [Yoda's passing is perhaps proof of General Douglas Macarthur's claim in the 1950s: "Old soldiers never die, they just fade away"].

Yoda's instructive self-sacrifice is not apparent in the film or script, however, in that he is portrayed as old, weak, sick and dying in despair. Vainly, he tells Luke he should look so good at 900 plus years of age. As a natural experience, death usually is less traumatic than birth (and the rest of life) for only the corpse remains and the living soul departs for heaven. Yoda says, "Twilight is upon me and soon night (knight) must fall. That is the way of things, the way of the Force."

Living Soul Departs

But perhaps Yoda appeals to Luke's vanity. Maybe he wants Luke to be okay with his transition and answers positively: "Do I look so old to your eyes?" Yoda wants to lighten the situation, for Luke is about to be orphaned for the fourth time: parents, foster-parents, Obi-Wan and now Yoda. The old sage knows death of the body is not the end of life and wants Luke not to grieve since he faces a bigger task — changing his mind to save "the world."

With Yoda's expiration, the issue of human immortality falls silent. Given the presumptive weakness of his unproven knighthood, Luke still misunderstands and stays invested in the illusion of the abandoned mortal self. He considers sin, guilt, fear, war and death to be real. He thinks he must "attack," "defend," "fight" and "defeat" his enemies to free the rebel race from bondage.

Holding on to "evil," however, is a way of hedging on transcendence. There is no reason for a split decision in a contest with God. Peace astronauts of the soul come and go as needed and appear extinct only in time but never in eternity. Their appearance may be invisible but their angelic function can never be terminated. The soul has no birth or death.

Luke is discouraged, but Obi-Wan comes quickly to console and counsel him, as usual, in the form of a spiritual visage. Luke confronts him with the deceit about his father and Obi-Wan equivocates: "What I told you was true from a certain point of view." Luke tells him that he cannot kill his father and begins to see himself in the image of his Father. ("Call no man on earth your father, for you have one Father, who is in heaven," *Matthew 23:9*).

Luke no longer regards himself as the offspring of evil, for he understands that morality is not inherited. Now a wise and peaceful knight, Luke sees residual good in his father. Obi-Wan dissents, claiming that if this is true, "Then the Emperor has already won. You were our only hope." But Luke knows he is not the last hope and presses for confirmation of a reputed sister. Luke guesses it is Leia and Obi-Wan tells him, "Your insight serves you well."

Obi-Wan then asserts that instinctual feelings Luke has about his sister are dangerous and he warns, "Bury your feelings deep down Luke, because they could be made to serve the Emperor." But the repression of guilt attracts, rather than repulses the "dark side." The Emperor also tells Darth Vader that Luke's "compassion for you will be his undoing," but it proves to be his greatest asset.

Guilt Attracts 'Dark Side'

THE EVIL EMPIRE ENDS

Return of the Jedi (1983) was originally entitled *Revenge of the Jedi*. According to an Internet *Frequently Asked Question List*, "Some promotional materials (movie posters, patches, etc.) were printed with that title. These materials are now collectors' items." Lucasfilm perhaps sought to avoid confusion with the vengeful plot of *Star Trek II: Wrath of Khan* (Paramount 1982).

Upon Yoda's passing, misconstruing his mentor's teachings, Luke soars away to carry out his mission of militant combat with his biologic and psychic father. But soon Luke's attitude changes, as he decides to restore his father to the good side, rather than subdue him as the leader of the bad side. To enable this, Luke has to dismiss the idea that evil exists anywhere, especially in his mind.

> *After the destruction of the first Death Star, the Emperor ordered the construction of a second planet-destroying space station even larger than the first. Assembled in orbit around the emerald moon Endor, the second Death Star is protected by an energy shield from the planet surface below. This titanic weapon is only part of an insidious plan to draw the Rebels into doomed combat, for the Death Star's incomplete structure hides its full operational capabilities and it is a giant trap waiting to fatally ensnare the Rebel Fleet"* (Texas A&M Website).

Project Hate & Provoke Fights

Luke flies to a giant redwood forest on an adjacent moon that looks a lot like Northern California. He joins pygmy bears, primitive teddy-bear-creatures who have a curious habit of wearing clothes over their furry skins. The rebel troops plan to attack the shield so that the armada of the alliance can destroy the second Death Star, symbol of renewed resistance to spiritual growth.

Luke meets Leia to inform her that she possesses mind power and that the two are siblings. To both bits of news she replies, "Somehow, I have always known." On the death sphere nearby, Darth Vader senses Luke's whereabouts. Luke realizes he endangers the mission, and tells Leia "there is good" in their father. He believes if he surrenders he will not be turned over to the Emperor. "I can save him and turn him back to the good side," he declares.

Luke sounds like Anne Frank (1929-1945) who hid in an attic with her family for two years, during the Nazi occupation of The Netherlands. In her famous *Diary of Anne Frank* she wrote the poignant lines, "In spite of everything I still believe that people are really good at heart." No one is so depraved that they cannot be saved by love and kindness. So, Luke submits to storm troopers without malice or militancy.

As a new peace master he realizes that armed conflict is pointless, and he passes through the final veil of darkness to demonstrate defenselessness. Luke stands vulnerably before the giant icon of evil, calls him "father" and moralizes that Anakin "is the name of your true-self. You've only forgotten. I know there is good in you." This means the good father, Anakin, never really died.

To illustrate his point, Luke reminds Father Vader that he was not able to kill him on the first Death Star at the end of *Episode IV*. Moreover, Luke says he knows his father will not hand him over to the Emperor, but he is soon betrayed. First, his father examines his reconstructed light saber and declares, "Your skills are complete. Indeed you are powerful as the Emperor has foreseen."

Standing before the chief executive officer of hate, Luke is told by the Emperor that he will be forced to capitulate to the "dark side" like his own father. A gnarled old man, hooded and robed like a ringside boxer, sits in the arena of the galactic ego as the undefeated champion megalomaniac. He represents the elderly, self-absorbed and disgruntled, fighting against death to the bitter end.

CEO of Hate

Luke insists that he will not turn to the dark side — will not be thrown in the throne room. Sparring verbally and posturing threats, the Emperor incenses Luke by annihilating rebel ships in battles just outside the window. Then Luke knocks his dad down, but realizes by fighting that he is going over to the "dark side." He stops dueling with Darth Vader and recognizes his father's (and his own) basic goodness.

The phantom enemy appears during fatal moments when the love of God seems absent. At first, like a scared child hiding from a wrathful parent, Luke disappears. But then in action symbolic of transformed resolve, he performs an amazing reverse somersault (adopting reverse perspective). He lands on a catwalk overhead, metaphorically in higher consciousness. With perfect vision, Luke now looks down calmly on his father without condescension.

As peacekeeper, instead of an outraged space fighter, Luke announces his new non-militancy. He must draw on inner resources to take this revolutionary new stance. Determined not to fight his father, but still fearful for his twin sister, Darth Vader is able to psychically read his "weakness," and for the first time, learns about Leia's existence. Characters who intuitively read each other's thoughts suggest being of one mind.

Self-Absorbed & Disgruntled Elderly

Darth Vader threatens to corrupt Leia saying, "If you will not turn to the dark side, then perhaps she will." Infuriated, Luke surges to retaliate, knocks his father to his knees, cuts off his right hand and disarms him of his will to fight for the "dark side." Thinking instead of acting, Luke insightfully repudiates violence by refusing to execute his father. Consciousness is the sword of the soul.

Sword of the Soul

Here the screenplay reads:

> *Luke looks at his father's mechanical hand, then to his own mechanical, black-gloved hand and realizes how much he is becoming like his father. He makes the decision for which he has spent a lifetime in preparation. Luke switches off his light saber. Luke casts his light saber away. The Emperor's glee turns to rage.*

Luke decides to open to the idea of good within himself. He does not attack but surrenders to the love of God and performs a genuine *coup de grace*. The bedeviled Emperor, however, steps in to unmercifully assail Luke with bolts of dark side lightning. Darth Vader looks back and forth between his gleeful master and his writhing offspring. For a moment, it appears, along with his weapon, that Luke has thrown away his life.

Genuine Coup de Grace

Unarmed, Luke lifts not a hand in self-defense. Near death, the electrified youth stretches out his arms in agony and pleads, "Father, please. Help me." Shocked by the Emperor's lethal cruelty, Darth Vader's dormant paternal instincts are aroused and he is restored to fatherhood, meaning he finds love in his heart for his suffering son. He grabs the Emperor from behind and like two mad wrestlers, hurls him into the shaft of the reactor furnace.

COUP DE GRACE: DEATH BLOW OF MERCY TO END SUFFERING.

FAITH & PEACE

GUILTLESS

Darth Vader hurls the awful Emperor out of the galactic arena of the ego into the abyss of oblivion, ridding his mind of evil. Without guilt there is no reason to project hate and provoke fights. So, his life as villain passes away and total good returns to rule the galaxy. He then briefly models peace consciousness.

The shafted evil sorcerer bursts into flames as the nucleus of the sphere explodes with the release of all its phony, pent-up energy. Dark forces betraying one another means everyone is striving hard for peace that is imminent. Faithless hostility disappears as rebels triumph in a graceful wisdom *coup d'état*. In franchised writings, the fantasy of the persistence of evil is confirmed as a crafty new clone Emperor shows up six years later.

Evil is Vanquished

To escape the morbid orb, Luke drags his father's hulk to a shuttle-craft as the fortress explodes in flames from attacks on its main generator by rebel fighters flying within its bowels. Breathing heavier than ever as a result of all this excitement, Darth Vader asks Luke to remove his mask and helmet. This means surely he will die. Becoming human, Anakin now says to Luke, "Just for once let me look on you with my own eyes."

A scorched, hairless, elderly man smiles faintly in recognition of his good self in the image of his son and dies a natural death with no fear. Without his mask and helmet he resembles his tormented kinsman (Jabba the Hutt). Luke illuminates, rather than eliminates his father and the two are resplendent in the end. Darth Vader dies as Anakin Skywalker. His last words are, "You were right about me being basically good. Tell your sister."

COUP D'ÉTAT: OVERTHROW OF THE STATE BY A SMALL GROUP.

Death Without Fear

Anakin dies a Jedi; sending a message of hope to everyone who thinks their "wickedness" puts them beyond redemption; more wicked even than Darth Vader? Father and son wrack Satan, rescue humanity and restore faith. The "evil" side of Anakin Skywalker, expires because good overcomes "evil" in Luke's mind. (As an officer in the Roman Army, persecuting Christians before converting to Christianity, the Apostle Paul established a precedent in self-forgiveness).

The grandiose ego cannot survive without its evil headmaster, who invents all the horror about death in the first place. Guilt and sin encircle your mind like a crown of thorns and you are made self-centered in pain, wanting only to retaliate. In the darkest corner of the mind, pacifists are persecuted as traitors to the custom of revenge. Pride and arrogance deny divine consciousness that is humble in having faith like a little child.

But why must Anakin die? His severed hand was artificial, so he felt no pain. Might he not have been healed psychologically and physically, and lived happily thereafter with his new understanding? Might not Anakin have returned to being a Jedi Knight? Is a sequel about a reformed terrorist-politician not viable commercially? Only Darth Vader's mortal body was wounded by the Emperor's "white lightening."

Betrayers of Revenge

Darth Vader's conversion proves that the darker the appearance of the knight, the brighter is the inner light. To be elevated to heaven, however, his remains must be consumed in a ritual baptism of purifying fire. While the victors celebrate, Luke cremates his father's carcass. That Ben and Yoda are master knights is the reason their bod-ies vanish when they die. But to liberate Darth Vader's soul, Luke must ignite a funeral pyre and bid farewell to an old enemy.

FAITH & PEACE

ANTICLIMAX

In the finale, Luke throws away his light saber saying, "I will not fight you, Father." Contrary to expectation and tradition, he does not slay Darth Vader in a climatic light saber duel. He refuses to be furious and assault the "dark side." He relies instead on mind power to bring about personal and universal peace. Bells toll a farewell to arms and all is quiet at the front.

The recovered soul of Lucifer (the Light Giver in Latin) flees back to heaven. He is then free to return as a new warrior or peace knight. Luke surrenders to mind power and no longer needs a civil war to keep guilt covered up with rage in his mind. This ending makes clear that *Star Wars* is ultimately an antiwar film and that Luke is a wisdom hero of peace. The universe is saved from the titans of death by a solitary youth who turns on Light consciousness.

Farewell Old Enemy!

All this comes to pass because Luke dared to recognize his immortality and bring down the heinous regime of corruption. Fireworks explode and alliance fighters fly overhead in a galactic independence day celebration. The rebel allies defeat the axis empire; Light forces conquer dark forces via consciousness. Luke looks lost, yet the venerated trinity, Yoda, Obi-Wan and Anakin, are joyful. This beloved board of immortals surpasses all ordinary heroes.

Lucifer = Light Giver

They nod in compassion at Luke's grief but are aware of the importance of his achievement from their divine elevation. And so it happens that peace perseveres, no longer just an interlude between galactic military campaigns. The "dark forces" can never be reconstituted because trusting in God dissolves sin, guilt and evil. When the Light is on your side and you are on the Light side, a victory is won through the law of faith.

Wisdom Hero of Peace

Allah and Shaitan

From: dreadnot@hotmail.com
To: jsnodgr@calstatela.edu
Subject: Re: "On Becoming a Jedi Knight"
Date: Thurs, 24 Jun 1999

As a Muslim I believe that there is only one true force, namely "Allah." All things, whether perceived as 'good' or 'evil,' form the 'light' or 'dark,' and manifest from His will. The choice determines who we are.

We are all Allah's evident 'slaves' but are not Shaitan's (the Devil's) eager disciples. The 'dark side' is just a label — it has no real power. All power is due to Allah. There is 'light' and there is 'no light' but darkness has no substance. The 'dark side' is just an imaginary form of the 'Light Side.'

Random individual violence and organized military warfare pervade human history. Luke's final stand repudiates the claim that an offended deity seeks penitence and retribution. And it repudiates the common secular custom of blood revenge: *lex talionis* (an eye for an eye and a tooth for a tooth). In his glory, Luke reaffirms the code of mystical knights that negates physcial force and restores the prime directive of faith in the force of God.

NINE

FEMALE KNIGHTS

In theatrical releases of *Star Wars*, Lucasfilm reports that thirty-five percent of the audience consists of women (starwarschicks.com). Yet, one question is inevitable — why are there no women Jedi Knights and why so few females in *Star Wars*? As leaders, Princess Leia and Queen Amidala have strong roles, but are overshadowed by the male characters. They are also disadvantaged in not being trained for knighthood.

Shmi Skywalker, young Anakin's mother in *Phantom Menace*, acts the part of a dupe, since her child is taken from her for the cause of war with her consent. He is only nine years old when he departs, and she tells him, "Be brave and don't look back." Perhaps "the system controlled her thinking," because she was just three years old herself when sold into slavery. Given the projection of mind power, outer forces appear to be real and absolute.

Returns to Love

Leia is a potential Jedi Knight but not trained, except in commissioned writings. Depicted as "feisty," she never protests the decision. The official *Star Wars Encyclopedia* patronizingly claims that her brother, Luke, taught her rudimentary skills. As the child of an authentic knight, however, the question is, why not? Does her sexual liaison with Han disqualify her due to guilt or is she just the wrong gender? The former involves her being physical, while the latter, her physical being.

Another question is — where in the galaxy is Luke and Leia's mother? From *Phantom Menace* we learn that she is Queen Padmé Amidala-Skywalker and that Luke and Leia will be born in *Episode III: Revenge of the Sith*. But why do the aunt and uncle raise the boy instead of his mother? We know the father is out raising hell, but what has happened to Lady Skywalker. The novel says she went to a peaceful planet with Leia, who remembers her mother there before she disappeared from the story.

There must be some reason beyond the lust for power that explains Darth Vader's denunciation of the Jedi Knights and dedication to the Evil Empire. Every novice gets frustrated and infuriated when knighthood does not come faster and easier, but they do not decide to embody the Anti-Christ. The absence of Padmé Skywalker-Vader in the sequel trilogy must be based on her assassination and that intensifies her husband's furious demise.

Refuses to Murder

In the finale to both trilogies, however, Darth Vader returns to love and refuses to murder his son, Luke. Is this achievement rooted in the childhood love of his mother, Padmé, as portrayed in *Phantom Menace*? His son, Luke, also exemplifies inner strength when faced with joining his father or leaping into the abysmal abyss at the end of *The Empire Strikes Back*. Was Luke able to "slay" his biological father and overturn his lineage, the result of the unconditional love of his mother and the Force?

GENDER & SEXUALITY

Spoilers: In *Revenge of the Sith*, Anakin will be banned from the Order of Jedi Knights for his affair and marriage to Padmé in *Attack of the Clones*. She will be assassinated in some gruesome fashion, probably by Jedi Knights and possibly even by Obi-Wan who "killed" Anakin Skywalker to unleash Darth Vader (Chapter 10).

Kiss = Sex = Sin

These tragedies accelerate Anakin's plunge into the black hole of the "dark side" where he eradicates Jedi Knights and tries to obliterate God. But his redemption at the end of the entire six-part *Star Wars* mega-saga, demonstrates that he never was trapped by evil — forever did it not control his destiny.

NAUGHTY KNIGHTS

Star Wars is known as an asexual film. "Lucas simply didn't want sexuality in his fairy tale," explained biographer Dale Pollock. Lucas perhaps wanted to appeal to younger audiences? Whatever the reason, Luke's romantic life is acted out discretely through the affair between Princess Leia and Captain Solo, his sister and best friend. Irvin Kershner, Director of *Episode V*, explained that in their love story, "A kiss is the equivalent of a sex scene."

The asexuality of Jedi Knights is conveyed by Yoda's innocent appearance. ("Yaddle" is a female version of Yoda on the Jedi Council in *Phantom Menace*, but there is no hint of romance between these two.) Similarly, Obi-Wan is depicted as a quiet old hermit living alone far out in the desert. During training, Yoda chastises Luke, "Adventure. Heh! Excitement. Heh! A Jedi craves not these things." To critics, *Return of the Jedi*, the climax of the classic trilogy, is the least exciting episode.

Lone Desert Hermit

That Jedi Knights are asexual is most evident, however, in the tragedy of their "extinction." Their legacy comes to an end when "their fire has gone out of the universe." Recruits are more attracted to physical fighting by the dark side, than to spiritual peace by the

Light side of the Force. Their vanishing involves some malfunction in spiritual reproduction and is not the result of being inadequate without mates and offspring. Meanwhile, Darth Vader sires twins of both genders and the evil empire multiplies.

Profane & Sacred Paths

Where does evil get its power and where have all the Jedi Knights gone, long time passing? Luke repeatedly is warned not to underestimate the "allure of the dark side of the Force." In an Internet article, *Star Wars Irresistible Force*, Kevin M. Nord links sexuality with the rise of the Dark Side when he states that "Anakin" might come from "Anakim," the name "in the *Old Testament* for a race of giants, 'the sons of the gods [who] lay with the daughters of men.'"

This myth alludes to the fact that even moral giants succumb to the temptation of bodily pleasure. An attraction to sensuality and an aversion to spirituality are commonplace also among mortals. Being aroused physically usually reinforces unconscious guilt in believing God condemns "sinful" behavior. Whenever guilt is hidden, the conflict is projected onto others who are seen as "evil." There are always self-attacks of guilt that underlie warfare.

Self-Attacks Motivate War

In *The Empire Strikes Back*, Luke decides to escape to battle during training when he encounters a second barrier to higher consciousness — the incompatibility of sensuality and spirituality. The first impediment is more conspicuous — he fears losing physical power and being vanquished by his foes. The second obstacle is the loss of eroticism and reproductive power, expressed in the more risque love story of Han and Leia.

Their affair ignites the moment Luke seeks a spiritual liaison with the ascetic Yoda. While Luke goes to spiritual boot camp, Han and Leia head for the cave of bestial delights and the two subplots unfold in back and forth cuts. Drawn to the ignoble Han, instead of the devout Yoda, Leia acts carnal rather than transcendental. She takes after her sexy father instead of the celibates Obi-Wan and Yoda. Leia also has no trainer and has lost her mother.

Forego or Go For Sex?

The sister follows the profane route and the brother takes the sacred path. Leia acquires a special love partner to offset the fear of death while Luke attempts pious transcendence. The first limits, but does not eliminate fear, while the second endeavors to surmount it morally. The split track between higher consciousness and romantic excitement divides the couple in the polarized world.

Both routes involve loving — the former with the mind and the latter with the body. Leia enters into a special partnership while Luke enters into a spiritual mentorship, two ways of contending with the grim reaper who harvests the father's hate through bloodshed and warfare. And, Luke quarrels with Yoda, just as Han and Leia bicker with one another, since both couples project the mistrust of the Force onto their mate. Neither way is superior.

Traditionally, one marries and has children while the other is sexually abstinent and joins a convent or priesthood. But if giving up sensual desire is the price to be paid for posting as a universal moral sentinel, no wonder young men and women everywhere recoil from peace duty and enlist instead for real military service. Then, like the pleasures of rest and recreation, sexuality compensates for the nasty business of war.

Fighting & Making Love

At their physical peak, young people are ready "to go for" rather than "to forego" sensuality. To give up earthly delights in exchange for celestial deliverance is an option for an elite corps of non-libidinous youth. Most people prefer making out, fighting and making-up to the boredom of celibacy and peace. The "couple's war" that follows the honeymoon period is also more thrilling.

Great Lover & Fighter

The opposition between spirituality and sensuality in *Star Wars* derives from the equation: "sex equals sin." This idea is woven into religious fabric and is the cloth of *Star Wars* theology. The rub is that one cannot be sensual without offending the deity and feeling shameful. Sex is then closeted in secrecy or eliminated in abstinence. "Sinful acts" must be hidden and one feels guilty — or desire must be repressed and one acts asexual — again overt and covert strategies that preserve the split mind.

Since a conflict is perceived to exist between moral knights and instinctual mortals, like priests and nuns in historical religions, Jedi Knights must remain chaste. Sexuality is thought to offend God, the way it antagonizes the asteroid beast in *A New Hope* (discussed in the next section). As a major inhibitor of vice and greed, faith is feared. So, the lower self opposes the higher self to preserve erotic behavior and to confirm the guilt is valid.

An action hero is usually a great warrior and a great lover, but a wisdom hero must give up both fighting and lovemaking. There is no liberation, however, when the decision for spiritual empowerment comes from sacrifice or sacrilege. True love knows no loss. To join the Force, young men and women think they must give up romance because it makes them guilty. Hence, the cadre of peace knights declines and the battle between good and evil is lost.

True Love Knows No Loss

Luke preserves his sexuality and he escapes basic training to rescue his compatriots. He flees to protect his masculinity that love making and fighting express. The fear of his feminine potential to surrender to the Force, however, is entirely unconscious. Dreading the loss of his masculine powers to fight and reproduce, Luke runs from Yoda's Principles 3 and 4, and returns to combat, reckoning that risking death is better than pledging lifelong chastity.

Historically, the clash between sex and spirit in religion required either vows of celibacy and also usually poverty, or sanctification through the custom of marriage. A less common method is to practice unique orgasm, i.e., "tantric sex." All three measures exaggerate the importance of sexuality, however, by making it acceptable only within certain bounds. Holy orgasm, celibacy and matrimony condemn other forms of sexuality as impious.

Join The Force?

Perhaps future installments of *Star Wars* can explore the association of sex and guilt when all the passion for fighting is spent. Advertised as "a love story," *Attack Clones* announced Anakin's transformation into Darth Vader. The love affair of Anakin and Padmé appears to cause the resurgence of the galactic war. The couple then repeat the fall of Adam and Eve that originated pain and suffering in the Western world. The link between sexuality and fighting, via the projection of guilt, is nowhere understood.

Star Wars modernizes, with color photography and special-effects technology, an old story told in black and white images, about good and bad people. Yet, the human habit of getting rid of hidden guilt, derived from substituting physical pleasure for spiritual love, persists in finding scapegoats to blame for the mistake. The realization that warfare arises from projected mutually denied guilt, in a covert mind war with God, provides some hope for peace on earth.

Romantic Tales

In the love story of Han and Leia, enmity exudes between the two when they first meet, that is aggravated by their social class differences. She is a well-bred princess from an aristocratic family. He attended a military academy and graduated with honors as an officer, but was discharged from royal naval forces for insubordination in defending mistreated slaves. He became a low-life smuggler and space pirate.

Fighting Lovers & Loving Fighters

That Leia is from a higher social class also suggests that she is further up the mountain of faith and is Han's leader in this domain (Chapter 4). As a mercenary in *A New Hope*, for example, he refuses to join the insurrection on the first Death Star, or to participate in Leia's rescue, unless he is well compensated. When he learns that she is threatened with termination, he says cynically, "better her than me."

A power struggle flares as their egos clash over who is in charge of the fight-flight plan, a ruse for who controls their relationship. Thus at first, there is a fight within the fight that divides their love from the larger cause. Given the logic of passion, the bigger the barrier between lovers, the more they are meant for one another and the greater their mutual desire. To truly love each other, however, they both must overcome their fear of being at peace with God.

When Han makes possible Luke's destruction of the Death Star (first rescue of Leia) at the end of *A New Hope*, he undoes his stigma of class inferiority and wins her affection. She witnesses his heroism that makes him eligible to be her suitor and their relationship is transformed from fighting lovers to loving fighters. No longer a degenerate outsider, but dedicated to saving rebel humanity, Han acquires the right to compete among insiders for her affection.

In the sequel, *The Empire Strikes Back*, their relationship regresses to bitter rivalry. Luke flies faraway to a swamp planet to train with his dry-witted mentor. Han rescues Leia with the aid of the crew and the droids, and they all escape Darth Vader's assault on their refuge. Han and Leia evade his pursuit by flying through an asteroid field to hide inside a cave on a giant rock hurling through space (second rescue of Leia).

In flight, the couple teases and speaks meanly to each other. Han refers to Leia as "your worshipfulness," and calling him "flyboy," she alludes to his basen mind and zipper. The cave actually is the interior of a giant space dragon, however. When the budding lovers think they are alone and safe, they share a first kiss. But an interloper, who is not jealous, See-Threepio, senses danger and foils their fun, pretending to investigate equipment repairs in their area.

Flyboy
=
Zipper

Their erotic interlude also arouses the beast, a stand-in for Satan, who is threatened by love from within his body even in its carnal form. Han narrowly flies the spaceship out of the hostile environment (third rescue) and is awarded kiss number two from Leia. It is rescue and reward, tit for tat, the merry merit pay system that entangles these two. No longer solo, Han gets a little more experience under his belt than his "younger brother" who is on an asexual trajectory to the Force.

Escaping the asteroid dinosaur, Han eludes Darth Vader again (fourth rescue) endearing him further to the princess and the whole band flies off to Cloud (Nine) City. Together in an apartment the following morning, Han takes payment again and kisses Leia for the third time. But the gang has been drawn into a trap set by Darth Vader, who wants to terminate Luke's training, the real threat to the empire, by resuming his fight with the "dark side."

Their sexual appetites activate guilt, sever the link with the Force and incapacitate even the faithful robots. See-Threepio is dismantled and Artoo Detoo is imprisoned. To prevent peace knight breeding, Darth Vader tests whether Han can survive carbon freezing before icing Luke. The love of Han and Leia goes beyond the sensual as she leads the ring of fellows to towers of faith. Without forfeiting physical love, you are drawn to peace via spiritual love.

The lovers biggest kiss (number four) comes just moments before the affair is cooled down by Han's petrification. At this moment, Leia declares for the first time, "I love you" and Han somberly replies, "I know." Perhaps he realizes that her love seals his doom. Or, he loves her but does not know if he will survive and so, does not try to convince her. Just as Yoda releases Luke during his death scene (Chapter 8) Han hides his love to free her to fight on.

Women Civilize Men

In *Episode VI*, Leia heads for the center of organized crime in outer space and with the warmth of her love, thaws Han out and continues to tractor him to the Light. Her rescue and masculine guise suggest that by falling in love, these two are complete equals. Immediately they kiss (number five) mutually and passionately for the first time. Any trace of rivalry is erased and they become amorous comrades. Their romantic bond is no threat to the Force that pulls the couple onward.

Embraced by love, but ignorant of their higher purpose, Han and Leia work together as paired rebel leaders, too occupied now for more kisses. At times, Han appears jealous of Luke's relationship with Leia. Following the destruction of the second Death Star, Leia informs Han that Luke is her brother and their competion completely vanishes. Since Han and Leia are not to be trained, there is no implicit vow of celibacy or other impediment to their union.

Love & Peace

As Leia's love for Han evolves over time, he is transformed from an egotistical rogue-outlaw into a champion military leader of the rebel cause. In mythology, women tame men by bringing them out of the wilds into civilization. Through love, Leia elevates Han's character, arousing passion for each other and devotion to the Force. In subsidiary materials they marry and the *Star Wars Encyclopedia* says Han becomes "the first husband of the New Republic." Following more kissing, they have three "Force-sensitive" children.

God may be expressed through sex, marriage and children, but spiritual wholeness does not depend upon these conditions. You do not

GENDER & SEXUALITY

BOUNTY OF LOVE

Disguised as a male bounty hunter, Leia rescues Han and they become commandos in the arms of love and war, kissing mutually and passionately for the first time, and uniting to fight evil forces in the galaxy. They represent the gender divided pair who take a secular route through romantic love to discover spiritual love, in contrast to Luke, who follows a direct spiritual path via training with his asexual mentor.

---

become complete, or incomplete, through physical union or commitment to another human being. Romantic love may be holy or unholy, but is not a prerequisite for peace knighthood. The Law of Faith involves consciousness of God no matter what is done with your body in time and space.

True romance erects barriers for lover's to cross to prove their mutual devotion. Because personal attachment often conflicts with military duty, *Attack Clones* confirms that love affairs are forbidden to Jedi Knights. (Sex before ballgames and battles may also deplete you). A taboo in the code of conduct stands in the way of Anakin and Padmé's true love for each other. Their affair and marriage break the rules, for which both are to be punished in *Revenge of the Sith*.

Separate trailers advertised *Attack Clones* as "Forbidden Love" and "Clone Wars." The cause and effect relationship between the two events, however, was not a message intended by Lucas. The themes correlate hidden shame with human strife, but moviemaker and moviegoer are not familiar with the idea that humans project self-attacks of guilt onto others in an undercover war with God. The lovers relationship must perish, however, for she is to be assassinated and he takes a dive into the "dark side."

Deep Spirit Phobia

In *Attack Clones*, testing Anakin's loyalty to the knightly order, Obi-Wan orders him not to rescue Padmé when she is imperiled. Given the continuous threat of her assassination, his near disobedience suggests that he will plummet into darkness in *Episode III* when she is killed as an advocate of love and peace. The deed must be done by Jedi Knights or republicans, for Anakin joins the Sith.

Anakin's turn to terrorism and the reactivation of the civil war, both follow their romantic affair and the consummation of their marriage. In the last scene of *Attack Clones*, Anakin breaks the code of celibacy of Jedi Knights to marry Padmé, his childhood sweetheart. That she is executed while he is banished, reveals gender discrimination and deep spiritual phobia.

In *Revenge of the Sith*, Anakin will turn to rage and rampage over her execution and his expulsion from the Order of Jedi Knights. Padmé's death will aggravate the suffering Anakin felt as a child when he was taken by the Jedi Knights from his mother for training. Anakin's three losses (mother, wife and community) will leave him with absolutely nothing to rekindle love in the tradgic ending to *Revenge of the Sith*.

Attack Clones also reveals that Anakin's descent into darkness is motivated by his guilt over having neglected his mother for many years. After being accepted for training at the advanced age of ten, another decade passes before he sees his mother again. He is too busy, like most young people, making his mark in the galaxy. He learns well the lesson of the Jedi Council in *Phantom Menace*: to not ever think about his mother (Chapter 10).

Anakin does not know she has been freed from slavery, has remarried, has a step-son, and has suffered "a hole in her heart" where he used to be (quoted from the novel). She dies minutes after their reunion and he goes berserk, slaughtering her kidnappers, including women and children. The novel states that Anakin misuses the Force to do his marauding. His neglect of her contributed to his mother's capture and torture, he believes, and aggravates the massacre of the nomadic tribe.

Clones Attack Themselves

It takes insight and courage to acknowledge that criticizing and assaulting others is always based on self-attacks of guilt. In departing Heaven, deep down we are all convinced of our own "original sin." Since politics arose historically to preclude intimacy with God, human beings habitually blame others for the desertion. The hidden guilt is then projected onto strangers and foreigners who deserve punishment for being different. The idea of attacking clones does suggest, however, that we fight no one but ourselves.

TEN

BUNCH OF SITHIES

The war in *Phantom Menace* is incited by a cartel of greedy businessmen and politicians who monopolize commerce in the galaxy. They blockade a peaceful planet ruled by a fair and good fourteen-year-old sovereign, Padmé Amidala (Natalie Portman). She is Anakin's (Hayden Christensen) future wife and Luke's future mother. The reign of corruption is led by "the Sith," a bunch you dare not call "sithies."

A trade embargo "shrinks the film to the scale of the 19th Century," wrote film critic Roger Ebert in the *Chicago Sun Times* (May 17, 1999). As the "back-story" to the classic trilogy, however, *Phantom Menace* is meant to foretell events in the Twenty-First or Twenty-Second Centuries. Closer to our period, *Phantom Menace* is thus Star War's "Book of Genesis."

ORIGIN & TRANSMISSION

The ruler of darkness is the hideous Darth Sidious, who looks and acts just like the future prosecutor of death, Emperor Palpatine (Ian McDiarmid). When tyrants have double names (Palpatine = Sidious and Dooku = Tyranus) and appear to be identical, in blue-tinged holograms, epoch after epoch, they must be fake. The "Lord of the Sith" has a red-devil apprentice, Darth Maul, precursor to the black-clad Darth Vader.

An Elected Queen?

Anakin is a gifted nine-year-old slave boy living with his single mother in poverty on a remote planet. Coming from a one-parent family and the lowest social class suggest that the origin of Jedi Knights has nothing to do with wealth or status. He looks to be five or six years old but the actor, Jake Lloyd, was eight at the time of filming. Reacting to a *Phantom Menace* poster in a toy store window, a mother was heard to exclaim incredulously to her son, "You mean that little boy becomes Darth Vader?"

On screen, the hero descends in age while off-screen, the film-makers ascend. Lucas claimed that *Phantom Menace* was designed for prepubescent boys and girls, as contrasted with the teenage target audience of the classic trilogy. Quoted in the *Los Angeles Times*, he added, "It is a film for twelve-year olds . . . a Saturday afternoon serial for children" (May 10, 1999).

Don't Call Me 'Sithie!'

"Annie" (not "Ani") is an expert "pod racer" and in close-ups, resembles a fierce kindergartner on a tricycle. Given his diminutive size and name, he appears to be androgynous. "Pods" are chariots without wheels propelled across the hot planet by pairs of big jet engines. Race scenes with diverse drivers and spectators depict the competition among ethnicities on this home world.

To make sure the audience gets the message, Anakin is the action hero of the film twice over. First, he wins first-prize money that pays for repairs to the queen's spaceship to resume its flight to the capitol planet. The second heroic feat occurs during the climax when Anakin accidentally pilots a space fighter, navigated by Artoo Detoo, to attack the command center of the invasion.

When the assault proves futile against deflector shields, the two sweep inside one of its hangers, launch two torpedoes and detonate the main reactor. The headquarters is demolished; suggesting that child-innocence naturally destroys evil. Padmé tells Anakin, "We owe you everything." The victory is fleeting, however, because Annie is not yet knighted and it occurs at the action level of racing and fighting.

The indisputable child-hero of the grand republic single-handedly obliterates the enemy of the people at the macro level of the universe. A little ray of light expanding from within whose name is Anakin, effortlessly abolishes the flying space fortress from the inside out. Closer to a true self as a young child, he easily disposes of fantasies of sin and injustice. Anakin also technically obeys Qui-Gon's order to stay hidden in the spacecraft.

The parallels between father and son, Anakin and Luke Skywalker, are evident in these battle scenes that remind us of Luke's assault on the Emperor's Death Star — to take place in future *Episode IV*. As the back-story, *Phantom Menace* tells how the father, Anakin, learned that evil prevails and must be eliminated in the galaxy. Luke learns his father's lesson as a child, for both are taught by elders that evil exists personally and universally (Chapter 10).

Officially, Anakin is scheduled to begin his fall from grace in future *Episodes II* and *III*. Luke and Leia are to be born after Anakin "dies," accidentally scalded to death by falling into a volcano of vicious lies and hate. Anakin did not know that Padmé was pregnant, nor that she eventually gives birth to twins: Luke and Leia. As Darth Vader, he unknowingly tortures his daughter about the site of a rebel base and almost kills his son in a chase during the conclusion to *A New Hope*

In *Episode I*, a crescendo of combat arises between Qui-Gon (Liam Neeson) and Obi-Wan (Ewan McGregor) who team up against Darth Maul (Ray Park) an apprentice crimson with animosity. Yoda claims two Lords of the Sith always appear together, master and apprentice, but here Darth Maul fights the two good knights by himself. Tattooed face, razor-sharp teeth, crown of horns and double laser sword, he demonizes adversaries.

Separation
→
Weak Body
→
Guilt
→
Fear
→
Hatred
→
Anger
→
Attack
→
Death
→
Loop

While a chorus sings *Qui-Gon's Noble End*, good and evil clash. The fight scene is beautifully choreographed inside a cathedral like structure. Darth Maul is more agile and fluid than the clumsy Obi-Wan. In the middle of the match, Qui-Gon kneels to pray to the Force. Because of it, the ending of *Episode VI* might have taken place right here and the serial would be over in *Episode* I.

But mysteriously, Darth Maul kills Qui-Gon. The distraught protégé, Obi-Wan, retaliates by slicing Darth Maul in half and the villain topples into the endless shaft of the "generator-melting pit," to be regenerated in many forms in future episodes. Darth Maul multiplies due to concentration on his destruction. Fighting evil is a "two-edged blade" — first you assume it exists and then you confirm it with efforts at eradication.

The clever master's "evil power" arises from guilt in the split mind of the dumb apprentice. Hating enemies reinforces the rule of guilt in your mind. "Evil" is overcome by disregarding it, not by opposing it. Hate separates you from God and you attack others because intensified shame makes you fearful of death alone without faith. Separation→ weak body→ guilt→ fear→ hatred→ anger→ attack→ death→ loop. Once you quit fighting you, however, war is over forever.

Chosen Child

Escaping her planet under attack, the Queen's damaged spacecraft lands for repairs on Anakin's home world. In an excursion into town to find replacement parts, Qui-Gon encounters young Anakin and quickly notices his dexterity, for example, that ordinary humans lack. Anakin is impressed in turn by a glimpse at Qui-Gon's big laser saber tucked beneath his poncho.

Father & Son

Each suspects the other of being a clandestine Jedi Knight and the secret theme of father and son emerges. From a portentous sand storm, Anakin invites Qui-Gon to his home for shelter and to meet his kind mother, Shmi Skywalker. The company is also introduced to See-Threepio, a robot Anakin has built for domestic labor. A child prodigy, Anakin is indebted to his mother for her loving protection in an alien slave system.

See-Thru-Pio?

See-Threepio now meets Artoo Detoo for the first time and is surprised to be told rudely that he is "nude," that is, has no metallic "body coverings." In biblical terms, he wears no "fig leaves." All his wiring, circuits and inner functions are entirely visible to everyone and symbolically, he extends Anakin's innocence. The endearing robot might have been named "See-Thru-Pio," for he has nothing to hide.

Anakin and See-Threepio have no secrets because without guilt, associated with sin, they are unashamed and know nothing of deceit. Anakin's loving mother shields him in a wanton world and preserves his natural purity. As a visionary, when they first meet, Qui-Gon tells Anakin's mother, "He's a very special boy." The novel adds, ". . . the look she gave him suggested they shared an important secret."

A Wanton World

According to the script, the mother reacts as if Qui-Gon has "discovered a secret." Apparently, Shmi is fully aware of Anakin's spe-

PRECOCIOUS ROBOT

Anakin confers his innocence on an emaciated C-3PO and constructs him "nude," that is, without body coverings. He might be called, "See-Thru-Pio." As a guiltless child prodigy, Anakin easily gets rid of hateful thoughts that save the galaxy from evil in *Phantom Menace*, as does his son, Luke, in *Return of the Jedi*. Luke throws his weapon away when he recognizes that evil is fantasy and warfare ends forever.

Prequel to the Prequel?

cialness and awaits his adoption by a teacher of truth. But the two adults act as if there is undisclosed information about the identity of Anakin's father. The introduction of a mystery about Anakin's ancestry indicates that we may need a prequel to the prequel — to return to an even earlier time for clarification.

Qui-Gon explains to Anakin's mother that quick reflexes mean Anakin sees events before they happen. Psychically gifted too, Qui-Gon foresees that Anakin will qualify as a Jedi Knight. Qui-Gon asks about Anakin's father and Anakin's mother says, "There was no father, that I know of . . . I carried him, I gave birth . . . I can't explain what happened." She then asks Qui-Gon to help her son, and in the novel, but not in the film, she touches his arm.

Phantom Seduction?

Is reproduction another function of the amazing Jedi Knight laser sword — perhaps the reason the rod hums and glows? (Its length is said to extend by turning small knobs on its handle). Shmi's statement may be taken literally or figuratively — an immaculate conception or an absconded father — a chosen or abandoned offspring? Qui-Gon reassures her that Anakin has "the way," but already "he's too old" for training. By comparison, his son, Luke, will be eighteen when he starts.

> Qui-Gon tests Anakin's blood while his mother, Shmi, observes from a doorway in her home. In a gesture of affection, Qui-Gon touches her shoulder, a departure from the script at the insistence of Liam Neeson, who played the role. The scene was retained only after negotiation with the director. These two are the parents of Anakin Skywalker who becomes Darth Vader?

Knight and Slave

Qui-Gon tests Anakin's blood for infection while treating him for abrasions after a competition. Qui-Gon notices Shmi watching from the threshold of a doorway as he discovers high concentrations of "midi-chlorians." According to the screenplay, she is "embarrassed" by the intimacy she reveals to him in her glance. The official *Making of Episode I* says there is a "hint of romance" and "subtle chemistry" in their relationship (Bouzereau 1999).

Hand & Shoulder

Because the test for midi-chlorians proves positive, Shmi is told that her son is to be released from slavery and taken to a distant planet for examination by an elder tribunal. Liam Neeson, playing Qui-Gon, departed from the script at this point, touching the shoulder of Pernilla August, the Swedish actress who played the role of the mother. From behind, he places his hand on her shoulder and asks, "Will you be all right (without Anakin)."

The gesture was allowed only after intense negotiations with Lucas according to media reports at the time of the shooting of this scene. Surreptitious tenderness and blood test results discussed in the home arouse suspicion that these two are the natural parents of little Anakin. Qui-Gon's culpability as progenitor would then explain his death (execution?) at the end of *Phantom Menace*. He has broken the celibacy code of Jedi Knights that foreshadows his son Anakin's future tie with Padmé.

A Touching Gesture

Creed vs Greed

Is paternity another one of Qui-Gon's personality quirks? Was *The Slave Mistress and the Jedi Knight* an episode of *Star Wars* not released in theaters? Like angels fallen among mortals, romantic tales might be told about Jedi with non-Jedi Knights? Anakin inherited his fascination for the opposite sex, his downfall in *Attack Clones*, from Obi-Wan, his father? An implication is that "evil" arises from the *miscegenation* of races or classes.

Meanwhile, Qui-Gon obtains his son's freedom but not his former mate's. He tells Anakin, "You are strong with the Force, but you may not be accepted by the Council" (because of age). "If you succeed," he warns, "it will be a hard life." Anakin turns to his mother and she tells him, "Listen to your feelings Annie, you know what's right." The mother thus encourages the child to trust his own mind and by implication, the Force.

Elder Tribunal

A schism between creed and greed paralyzes the galactic congress. While the Queen pleads with its leaders to defend her planet, Qui-Gon petitions the elder tribunal to approve Anakin's training and to assign him as the trainer. Qui-Gon is not a member of the elite clergy in the "Temple of the Jedi" because his thinking is too strident. His chief detractor, Yoda, Council Grand Master, is a younger, greener, feistier, hairier critter than in previous episodes.

Anakin is brought to be character tested before the board of twelve master knights who gather in a circle. Three are female and two of these are human. Yaddle is a third female who appears to be of the same species as Yoda. Mysteriously in this episode, *Attack Clones*, the females disappear and we never see the interior of the whole chamber. Female Jedi Knights show up later, however, for the first time ever, in gladiator battle scenes.

MISCEGENATION: SEXUAL INTERCOURSE OR MARRIAGE BETWEEN RACES OR CLASSES.

Yoda interrogates Anakin and given the way he is treated, Anakin complains that he feels cold. Yoda reprimands him saying, "Your thoughts dwell on your mother" and "Afraid to lose her . . . I think." Defiant, like his father, Qui-Gon, little Anakin retorts, "What's that got to do with anything?" Yoda then pontificates, "Fear is the path to the dark side . . . fear leads to anger . . . anger leads to hate . . . hate leads to suffering."

Humility & Humanity?

Wanting to live up to senior council expectations, but fearing he will be rejected for training and disappoint Qui-Gon, young Anakin insists, "I'm not afraid." In conduct unbecoming to a sage, Yoda acts like he believes the cadet, instead of trusting his own fabled intuition and resumes the interrogation. Yoda acts cruel and provocative. What has happened to his humility and humanity?

Yoda is fearful of Anakin becoming a Jedi Knight and the chief conveys fear, root of all aggression, to the plebe. A little slave boy, without a legal father or future, is taken from his single mother to an inquest by strange creatures on a faraway planet and challenged not to be afraid? Yoda acts like the commander in chief of the armed forces of the Jedi, the role he actually adopts in *Attack Clones*.

Living under a harsh system of slavery, Anakin has no identity of his own and, therefore, every reason to feel fearful. In interviews, Lucas reported to the media that shooting the goodbye "was a difficult scene" because Anakin was supposed to be upset about leaving his mother but not distraught. According to the novel, however, "tears streaked his face" and he was "wracked with sobs."

The Chief Conveys Fear

Spoilers: Padmé's love eventually soothes the trauma, but their affair and marriage break the sex taboo that leads to Anakin's expulsion from the community of knights. She must hide her pregnancy and her babies before being executed in *Revenge of the Sith*. For her to be murdered by Obi-Wan would be the ultimate betrayal of the original friendship with Anakin.

Scared & Scarred

Without compassion, the elder tribunal tests Anakin's ability to conform and forbear pain. Why are these super-intelligent beings insensitive to his plight and why is it wrong to complain and be fearful? Historically, the endurance of pain is part of an induction test into war culture. The elder tribunal initiates Anakin to the "dark side." Officially, his descent begins in *Episode II*, but he is scared — and scarred — here in *Episode I*.

Because it is one mad cycle, the process also works in reverse. Fear creates the judgment of sin that justifies withholding kindness and permits the intimidation of others. Smart children sense the insane system of sadism, but are not able to rebel until puberty. As adults, however, they can exercise their free will, break the historical chain of violence and find peace consciousness.

In *Phantom Menace* there is no victory celebration, however, because Qui-Gon is gone (dead). Anakin's only ally is killed and the child is stripped of mother and father, in a process identical to the one to be endured by his own son, Luke, orphaned four times in sequel episodes. Ranking officers in a culture at war with "evil" immerse Anakin in anger and fear through separation from his mother, threats of rigorous training and a heartless endurance test.

Orphaned Four Times

Yoda notices Qui-Gon's defiant streak in Anakin and therefore does not approve his nomination for training. Yoda senses "grave danger" in the proposal to train Anakin and Yoda speaks for fear, anger, hate and suffering by opposing the child's potential to succeed. The master council does approve, however, and the matter is settled temporarily. Obi-Wan tells Anakin, "I am your Master now. You will become a Jedi, I promise."

Before credits roll, however, alluding to the endless spin of violence, Yoda deliberates as to whether it was the insidious Darth Sidious or malicious Darth Maul, apprentice or master, who was

PUSHED FROM GRACE? Anakin Skywalker, proto hero and proto villain of *Star Wars*, is subjected to fear and anger in an endurance test in *Phantom Menace*. As a slave child, he is separated from his mother, brought before a panel of strange creatures and challenged not to be afraid. Hazed in a right of passage, the cadet is introduced to the "dark side" by a forum of senior officers in a culture at war with evil. Here begins his transformation into Darth Vader. Officially, his final fall is scheduled for *Revenge of the Sith*.

---

slain by Obi-Wan. It matters not, because the ending is the beginning, in a non-stop cycle, whenever fighting sin is made an absolute good. In *Return of the Jedi*, not fighting is the inspiring last chapter of the mega-saga, the extraordinary ending to what gets started here in *Phantom Menace*.

Child Scalded in the Furies of the 'Dark Side'

You can disclose the ending of a series in the beginning because there is only one story to tell over and over. A wondrous boy-child deposes "evil" in the galaxy. Under the aegis of his mother, Anakin is brilliant, virtuous and courageous — until meeting outsiders (Qui-Gon, Yoda and the senior council) who scald him in the furies of the "dark side." As a minor and a slave, he learns that danger is real and it appears to be true.

Never was there, never is there, nor will there ever be, however, any evil that is real. Like children, we need to hear this story over and over. It is the same ancient story — because it is the one and only true story. When faith in God endures, only good prevails in time and space. Evil must be phony, or the title of this episode would have to be *Real Menace*. The myth in *Star Wars* is the fabrication of a "dark side."

Conspiracy

Sage or Savage?

In the next episode, *Attack Clones*, enemies are assaulted "justifiably" to conceal the fear of peace. Yoda becomes the commander of a clone army that fights the secessionists and leads a massive military invasion by Jedi Knights. Viewers are bombarded with special effects and cheer loudest when Yoda discards his cane to wield a weapon. "Gandhi turns Rambo," quipped *Time Magazine*. *The Matrix Reloaded* also exploits fighting and special effects in the transitional middle segment.

Replacing Jar Jar Binks, See-Threepio, beloved multi-lingual ambassador of universal peace, becomes the butt of comic relief. Accidentally, the robot's head is attached to the torso of an enemy battle-droid, suggesting that fighting now has lost all reason. Both robots are hysterical but harmless. Audiences go wild thinking the plight of the pair is hilarious, but the human species is ridiculous. Wisdom is a casualty missing in action.

Wisdom Missing in Action

Previously slandered by fans and critics alike, Jar Jar's diction has improved and his role as buffoon has diminished in this episode. He now serves on the staff of Senator Padmé Amidala and proposes to the ruling assembly that their leader be given absolute power to prosecute the war. The decoyed dictator will take over the empire in the next installment. Set up to betray the republic, claims by reviewers that Jar Jar Binks is rehabilitated are premature.

Senator Amidala is the only voice for peace and to her peril, opposes the building of a clone army for the defense of the republic. War advocates want fighting to resume no matter who wins or loses. Led by Yoda, the elder tribunal maneuvers Padmé out the political arena to protect her from plots of assassination that are provoked by their rivalry for power. Jedi Knights are thus implicated in the leadership of the Sith.

For example, Jedi Knights requisition the clone army now commanded by Yoda. The elder tribunal assigns Anakin to protect Padmé at an elegant retreat without supervision. He courts her and the peace initiative disappears from the debate, the way females are gone from the inner council chamber and the clone-production planet vanishes from celestial charts. The patsy, Jar Jar, takes her place and nominates the future tyrant. "Only a Jedi could do this," is a phrase that punctuates the film.

A Joint Conspiracy?

The Jedi Council appears to switch sides and collude with the Sith in the takeover of the galaxy. Using separatists as a front, the republic apparently is divided by Yoda and Palpatine for control by Jedi Knights and Sith in a joint conspiracy. The least suspicious figures, Obi-Wan, Captain Typho and See-Threepio, all claim this puzzle is not logical. But is it illogical to suspect that Jedi Knights, *en masse*, have capitulated to the dark side?

In the novel, a bounty hunter teaches his clone-son that the art of deception lies in appearing to do one thing while actually doing another. The boy pretends to fish while learning deceit from his father. The father appears to relax with his son while overseeing the assassination of Padmé. Jedi Knight leaders appear to be peacekeepers while instigating war. Just as the assassin is assassinated, conspiracy camouflages conspiracy. Yoda reiterates, "Unseen is much that is here."

Conspiracy Camouflages Conspiracy

It is Palpatine who suggests to Yoda, who consents, that Jedi Knights guard Padmé. She is "protected" as the senate opposition leader who might discover their collusion? It makes no sense for separatists, or Sith, to assassinate her since she supports their cause by opposing an army that would fight them. When Padmé asks Yoda in the novel, "Who's behind it," he does not answer, just as he does not reply when Obi-Wan wants to know if he requisitioned the clone army.

A Tactile 'Body Guard'?

The Jedi Council suspends Anakin's supervision by master Obi-Wan. Replacing Padmé's security captain, Anakin is authorized to do nothing but "guard" her. Further, Palpatine and the senate prohibit Jedi Knights from investigating separatist discontent that might uncover republican corruption and the link to Jedi Knights. Yoda dismisses Obi-Wan in an interview when trainees hypothesize that the clone manufacturing location was erased from the archives by insiders.

The elder tribunal ignores Obi-Wan's reservations about Anakin's reassignment, just as Obi-Wan pays no attention to Anakin's complaints about not being permitted to pursue the assassins (though delighted duty puts him together with Padmé). Anakin is correct — he is not given his master knight trails for fear he will be independently minded like his father, Qui-Gon, and discover the conspiracy of Jedi Knights? For copulating with Shmi and conceiving Anakin, Qui-Gon was clandestinely executed in *Phantom Menace*?

Hunting assassins, Obi-Wan discovers the manufacture of clones for an army ordered by Jedi Knights. Practicing deception, he pretends to inspect the project as part of his research. He finds out that a Jedi Knight who left the order is suspected (Dooku) but one reportedly killed (Dyas) actually signed the contract that is brokered by bounty hunter Fett. The broker was awarded clone-template and clone-child as bonuses for agreeing to kill Padmé?

Obi-Wan acts naive about the conspiracy when questioning the bounty hunter, who then realizes that he is being double-crossed by the Jedi Knight leadership. With his clone-child in hand, he tries to flee to separatist territory. Ordered by the elder tribunal to take him into custody, however, Obi-Wan attacks first: breaking the already shattered Jedi Knight code of conduct, endangering the child and implicitly joining the conspiracy.

Dooku is Yoda's former Padawan and reputed to be one of the greatest Jedi Knights of all time, whose bust is still on display in the library. The chief archivist (Nu) and Yoda's lieutenant (Windu) frankly defend Dooku, presumably based on their insider knowledge about the moral corrosion of the leadership of Jedi Knights. Dooku warns Obi-Wan that the republic is under Sith control and openly invites him to join their revolt.

Spoiler: Is Count Dooku a double agent leading separatists while secretly re-establishing the moral integrity of the traditional order of Jedi Knights? He fights with a light saber in a superior style long out of fashion. He will be eliminated by Anakin in *Episode III* to make possible the understudy of Emperor Palpatine (according to shadow.com). Leading the *Revenge of the Sith* as Darth Vader, he will wipe out the Jedi Council in retaliation for the order to assassinate Padmé.

Spoilers: An advance, underground Internet plot summary claims that Anakin discloses the corruption of Jedi Knights to Padmé. She believes and supports him, and he continues to love her. Thinking she has led Obi-Wan to him, however, Anakin is enraged when she appears at the start of their legendary duel. Anakin "Force chokes" her and she hits her head as she falls. Anakin is mutilated after slipping into a volcano and Obi-Wan rescues Padmé. But she becomes gravely ill and dies on his escape vessel (shadow.com). In another version, she dies at the scene (allscifi.com).

That Jedi Knights have joined the Sith is heresy to most *Star Wars* fans. You either embrace *Attack Clones* as an enthusiast or critique the film as a reviewer. The Force Net (forcenet.com) an unofficial *Star Wars* website, for example, found the author's review of *Attack Clones* to be "incendiary." The two-part essay was published online by Film Threat (filmthreat.com) a website on the Internet devoted to independent thinking and filmmaking.

Mirrors Split Thinking

That Jedi Knights lead the Sith and betray their original mission to save the galaxy is not an argument designed to antagonize *Star Wars* fans. In fact, it dissolves all the battle lines, including the one between devotees and critics. The creation of enemies occurs by the projection of self-hate that is unconscious (like the missing location of the clone-producing planet in the movie). The director himself is not aware of the conspiracy within the conspiracy in his own film.

Good guys are bad and bad guys are good, as mirrors of the hidden split in human thinking. When guilt is denied inwardly, however, the division into bad and good shows up outwardly, attributed to others who project it outward also. Clone attacks are always assaults of guilt that look like armies of enemies as long as the division is concealed. War is mutually projected self-hate denied.

As another example, in the *Spider-man* series of films (Columbia Pictures 2002, 2004) Peter Parker (Tobey Macguire) is openly divided between an or-dinary adolescent (*Spider-man*) an ordinary young adult (*Spider-man 2*) and the super-human figure of Spider-man. The more basic division into the Green Goblin (Willem Dafoe) and Doctor Octopus (Alfred Molina) as the hidden negative dimension in his personality is not portrayed.

War = Mutual Self-Hate Denied

Because they are not given recognition, these villains act outrageous, vindictive and cruel in the films. The 'dark side' thrives when guilt can live fully exposed in flagrant action (or hidden in shameful inhibition). You can be as bad as you want to be on the 'dark side' and even teach Darth Vader a lesson or two about being evil. With your big ego and great stubbornness, your guilt looks really valid to you and God is mistaken.

Because he espouses love, Peter Parker cannot marry Mary Jane Watson (Kirsten Dunst) because it puts him in danger of being killed by Spider-man's enemies. And, human beings cannot stop fighting each other until they begin to accept that the villains are split-off and denied parts of their own personalities. In "*Spidey 2*," Peter Parker works as a photographer, but his personality remains fragmented. He never gets the big picture because his camera (rational consciousness) stays focused externally.

Rage Rules the 'World'

Jedi Knights and Sith merge out of the joint fear of peace — an idea often deemed preposterous. Peace arouses a greater fear than being killed in warfare — the dread of eternal punishment by God for not having loved Him previously. As calm sets in, defense budgets and troops are allocated to provoke yet another war. Peace never lasts long because fighting re-erupts to keep the fear suppressed with anger that is rationally justified as defense against aggressors. Planets from all directions in the galaxy are drawn into brawling for yet another century.

Critics complain that Padmé's costumes "appropriate her natural beauty" but her gorgeous advocacy of peace in *Episode II* threatens to stop the fighting among rival factions (of the self) making one vulnerable to God's love. It is the message, not the person, who is feared and purged in reel time and real time. Faith in a higher power can reconcile hostilities between ancient enemies and make deadly force obsolete in all human relations. Without faith, however, rage appears to rule the 'world.'

Ready to Enlist

Date: Thur, 05 Aug 1999
From: "Sin Sin" sin2@hotmail.com
To: jsnodgr@calstatela.edu
Subject: I Want to Be a Jedi!

Hello, are you a Jedi Knight? If you are then will you tell me your Jedi name? Also, can you teach me how to become a Jedi? E-mail me back.

P.S.: I am 12 years old, how old are you?

Eleven

The Phantom Fiend
Mariano E. Meléndez

Robot

I am a male in my late twenties. I stand six feet and change; have dark hair, dark eyes, dark skin and weigh upwards of two hundred pounds. I have a high, narrow forehead, as was the style in the Victorian era among the aristocracy. I walk with a strange gait.

Who am I? Where to begin? I am born. I grow up. I die. Yes, die. I died about three years ago with the passing of my mother and the breakup with my fiancé. I saw my mother die and I also watched the love of my life speed away in a cloud of indifferent automobile exhaust. Since then, I have been living another life far removed from what I knew before.

I came into this world in the filthy city of Washington D.C. in the year 1972. While studying law my father worked for a senator. My mother taught high school and earned yet another degree in world history.

I recollect being strapped in a yellow high chair in the drafty breakfast nook near the kitchen. A screwdriver hung on the opposite wall — its handle was a beautiful deep blue — its shaft a most brilliant metal. The whole universe existed in that fascinating object. It was so far away — something unattainable. I guess I already knew something was screwed.

Fast forward to the City of Angels, an oxymoron. My sister is born and brought home to our small house — the year is 1976. She was all big eyes and waving hands. Joy permeated the living room and with amazement my parents looked down at my sister and smiled. They looked down at me and smiled.

With my Lego set spread across the dining room floor, I was about to embark on the construction of a new and more threatening robot when my sister lurched toward me. Gingerly, I cleared a path for her to make her way and waited patiently. Of course, my parents found this adorable, but I just thought it only logical. I do not know if this was the last of my genuine displays of consideration for others and the beginning of my lifelong indifference.

My father became a government lawyer and transferred to Arizona. I always have had an affinity for water in any form. My sister and I picked days so unbearably hot it hurt to open our eyes. We immersed ourselves in the Jacuzzi and then leapt out, dashed ten feet to the pool, and in gales of laughter, the icy water melted the heat from our bodies.

Arizona is the last memory I have of being truly happy. Back in Los Angeles, I finished high school and confronted that specter for the underachiever — the local community college. I was too smart for my own good and willingly embarked on a path toward self-destruction. Books, not peers and television, were the source of my corruption.

I reveled in the works of the narcoticized heroes of the thirties — Howard Phillips Lovecraft, Robert E. Howard and Clark Ashton Smith. These kindred spirits, were visionaries, geniuses and scoundrels, who evoked beauty and horror. Yes, these were the debauchers, ravagers, kings of the silver flask, imbibers of opium; tragic intellectuals among the damned.

Thus, began my decadent descent. Months? Years? I know not. I drank oceans of liquor, licked sheets of lysergic acid and snorted highways of powdery white lines. Endless nights were insulated from reality. I was searching for my muse, wanting to be the Hunter S. Thompson, the Jerry Stahl, the William Burroughs of the Nineties.

The only thing I found in those dark nights was this: the inner workings of cities are greed and despair. Evil pulses in the veins of the alleys, pubs, whore houses and bottles. I was on a sojourn in Hell. I was both the mad Doctor Faustus and the evil Mephistopheles.

Lover

Then I met my teenage angel of mercy. It was the tumultuous time of the World Cup. Disturbances broke out, windows were shattered, people marched up and down the streets brandishing flags from other countries and cursing in foreign tongues — an overall air of menace — and enter the soccer hooligans.

I saw her with some faceless friends in a café waiting out the mock riot. We met eyes, we locked eyes, I fell in love. We kissed that night, for the first time. I will never forget how utterly absolved I felt. She was a catharsis of beauty. I knew then I wanted to be with her forever.

We were still honeymooners, secure in each other and I was almost happy. There was one thing though — I was still Faustus. To keep this gift of heaven, I had to become a better person. I tried to reform but became a shadow and knew not myself anymore.

She was elated. She spoke of marriage, children, houses and marital bliss. I was all for it! But, I was not happy because she had no idea she was in love with a golem. To quote Richard Lewis' character in the film, *Drunks*, "it was so ...ing true you couldn't even say it."

I had to improve, so I joined the military. Wow, I leapt right in! The Navy, Special Warfare, Explosives and Ordinance Disposal, Special Combat, Aggressive Reaction Systems, Underwater Demolition and my favorite, Close Quarters Combat.

But this new kind of hell was not making me a better person. My angel began to lose interest and wanted out. Christ, I was doing it for her! One more thing, my mother was slowly dying of cancer. I came home. My fiancé left me. My mother died. I died.

I became one of my long-forgotten Lego robots. I functioned mechanically but did not self-destruct. Dante and Faustus both found their woman, but I was just a ruined fiend. I remember only indescribable sorrow. The day my mother's died, I recall my sister saying, "and so, I guess its over for you now." Was she right?

Scholar

Now we're here in real time. I enroll in the university and to my surprise, enjoy it. At times, the curriculum is insultingly below me. It is a nice, safe, predictable place. I am a student known by my social security number. Killing for the government are far behind me and my heartbreaking losses are overtaken by academic goals.

Still, I feel like a robot, but one with an old soul. I exist among teenagers with petty problems: "My parents won't let me stay out late!" "Gosh, "I drank six whole beers last night and I'm kind of sick!" "My girlfriend is cheating on me!" "My friends are pressuring me to try pot!" "I need my own place!" "These classes are too hard!"

Sometimes I don't know how I keep on trying to become a better robot. One more year and two quarters, and I am finished. Then it is off to graduate school. I am an anthropology-archaeology major — the most humanistic of the sciences and the most scientific of the humanities.

So far, I've been disgustingly successful in this endeavor: Honors Society and secretary of the Anthropological Society. I look forward to a doctorate in Egyptology and going to Cairo. The hot desert nights are made habitable by soothing beer in smoky taverns, rife with opium, and belly dancers in exotic silks.

Maybe that shinny blue screwdriver is within reach? Oh yeah, I am currently employed by Warner Brothers Television Studios in Burbank. Isn't that ironic? I live by myself in a one-room apartment in an esthetically challenged area of the city. I listen to Forties era music or Eighties punk rock. I read all the time and on my sacrosanct weekends I go down to the coast to surf.

SURFER

When I enrolled in this class, I was barraged by radical ideas and baffled. Most of us were. You waste no time. The concepts got harder to accept and down right outrageous at times. I believe that I speak for most, since I have stolen glances around the room and seen classmates as lost as me.

But some ideas stimulated a vision about my unrealized potential. I was determined to grasp the tenets, especially Principle 3: Phantom Enemy. The more I strove, the more understanding eluded me. Only now do I realize that I lacked willingness. That's all — mere willingness. The revelation came at the end of the quarter when I finally arrived on the marshy training planet.

You said, "Every morning we wake up to enter an insane asylum." I thought, "What!?" To paraphrase, you said that if we were to go into an actual asylum and inmates cursed or slighted us, we would pay it no mind. We would expect this behavior from the psychotic — insults would be shrugged off as meaningless — we'd know they are phantom curses.

You went on to say that society-at-large is the asylum but we don't see the sign over the gates. There is no partition — it is just one big loony bin. If we switch our perception, we will see the marquee announcing, "Now playing indefinitely: *The Insane World.*

We would see reality for the first time for what it is — a mere illusion. We would see our interaction with others and our feelings about ourselves, as products of dementia. We are visitors on tour through the crazy house — this all made sense to me — and it rested only on my willingness to see it.

Here is an example of Principle 3 in action. This weekend I went to Paradise Beach with my cousin. This part of the coast is rife with localism — all the bleached blond surf-punks know each other and who is an outsider. That day they were more hostile than usual. How can they lay claim to waves that are free? Sure, they live around there but the ocean is damn well not theirs.

They snaked waves that I had already dropped-on, cut in front and gave me menacing looks. I knew that I was in no real danger. They wouldn't take it that far. But I was still upset. I knew their taunts were merely feelings of inferiority that coincide with my own ideas about myself — where I live and the color of my skin. It was baseless and I let them roll away with the current.

I could wait out their wrath. Just so! They ran out of steam and left in a huff seeing that I was still in the water. I gave them a big smile and waved goodbye without any hint of malice. "See ya next week, fellas," I said. But I knew they never were really there to begin with, were they? And for me they would never be there again.

For the rest of the day, until twilight mingled with the salty air, I surfed waves I still dream about. It was just me and one or two of the old-timers, with the maturity to nod at me in greeting and go about enjoying our waves. Thank you for the initiation in training and someday I'll sign up for the rest of the course.

I Am SITH Lord
Lucho Guerrero

Free Fall

On August 4, 1977, a boy named Lucho Guerrero was born in Los Angeles. His parents were immigrants from México. He attended Catholic school and teachers were bothered by his lack of effort. Some accused him of not paying attention in class. He did not like boring games and sat with his friends talking about taking revenge on those awful nuns.

Lucho was expelled and went to public school. He breezed through high school and graduated doing enough work to get by, but never enough to get good grades. In high school, his goal was to have as much fun as possible: going to parties, cutting class, drinking and using drugs. Lucho was obviously a bad influence on himself and his friends.

He hurt his parents disobeying them. He came home late, drunk or high, or did not show up until the next day. He knew they would not throw him into the streets. Then he was accepted to college and was enthusiastic about going. Surprisingly, he did well and his family was impressed. But one warm Fall evening, two males pulled alongside his car, pointed a chrome pistol and shot Lucho.

I had a life like everyone else. I knew successful people and many who were the opposite. I was one of the successful ones. I was very content with my life. I was working hard and going to school. **I had it all . . . I Had It All!** I was big and strong. I was not afraid of anything.

Then some cold-blooded bastard decided to strip it all away from me. He shot several times. But he only got one in me. The son of a bitch waited to see if I got up. But I played dead. Not knowing I had been wounded, I quickly tried to leave in my car after he left.

While sitting in the car still in shock, I felt warm. When I looked at my hands and shirt I was drenched in blood. This was not a movie and there were no retakes. I screamed for help but only hot air came out of my mouth. No voice. Suddenly, a crowd was around me.

The fire department ripped the roof off my car. Damn, I really liked that car! So much time and money I put into it. It was taken away just like that! I was in the hospital for months, suffering humiliation having to be fed like a baby.

I could not even write. I had to go to the bathroom with someone. My hands hurt every day because of the nerve damage. I lose my balance often. My arms are incredibly weak. I lost my job and missed school for a full year. Then came the worst news of all.

I went to physicians and endured many degrading procedures. I have failed at everything. I had never touched a woman. I felt stupid for not taking my chance while I could. I am as innocent as a priest. Now I blame the world for bringing down my glorious empire.

Mangled

I see the world as traitor. I was always a good person. Other people's suffering now makes me feel better. Many of my relatives are trying marriage, family and children. But I want them to fail hard so they will know what it is like to suffer. I wish the worst for them. How dare they insult me with their successes!

A new Lucho was born a cripple, who looks deformed, with a heart full of hatred and rage, and a mind set on revenge. The only thing I think about is pay back. Who is responsible for this outrage? Perhaps fate was envious that he had gotten away with so many things in his life until then.

Someone wanted to assassinate him? Or, was it plain misfortune, being in the wrong place at the wrong time? Who knows? The truth will one day surface and this atrocity that devastated his mind and body will be over. Until then, Lucho will never be at peace.

We live in a world where there are good people and bad. Most people lead lives that have meaning. They have dreams and goals that may not be reached but still, they make the best with what they have. These are the mature ones.

Knowing there is no enemy, one can live fully and happily. JEDI, Justly Evolving and Developing Individual, is an idea I have found interesting. I now see *Star Wars* from a different angle. Though I understand you, I cannot accept this way of thinking.

I refuse to believe. I am not developing. I do not think I will ever be ready. I have thought about my dark future and have concluded that I am a Suffering Individual Through Hatred, or SITH. By twisting your idea my way, I can explain myself. What better way to do this than the nemesis of the Sith Lords?

I am not WILLING to become a better person, much less have any PATIENCE. I have too many ENEMIES to deal with. I hate almost everything in this world. Since I am suffering, I want the rest of the world to suffer just like me. I feel like death is grinning at me and enjoying it.

I know the routine. To become mature there are four steps. First, you must have the will to change and the least bit is enough to get you started. Second, patience, one must wait while development takes placet. The third step is to realize there is no enemy.

When Luke was put to the test in the cave, Darth Vader attacks him first. Vader is the aggressor and Luke must defeat him to become a Jedi. The fourth step is the power of the mind. Yoda explains to Luke that nothing is impossible but Luke has doubts.

I see life though my "injured self" because I really am injured. Now maybe you will understand a little bit more about why I cannot see a bright future. The last thing I found out was the most devastating of all. It is something that no doctor or Jedi mind-trick can solve.

This is why I will grow old, lonely and cold. No one wants a boy. A man I will never again have the chance to be. That opportunity I missed several times. I understand what is required but not everyone can be at peace. *I am a Sith Lord.*

CHINA DOLL
Mui Lam

DRAGON SLAYER

I am a Chinese woman bound by tradition and rules. I am quiet, obedient and patient. I am sensitive to criticism because I do not have high self-esteem. I also do not criticize other people. I try to be optimistic about life but always end up pessimistic. I am superstitious and do not like to rely on others.

I was born on July 16, 1978 in Hong Kong, the middle child in an immigrant family. There are seven in my family, my parents and five children. We came to America when I was five-years old. Being female and the middle child has always been a big disadvantage.

Growing up in a traditional Chinese home, I was taught to be respectful and well mannered. When I was little, my mother dressed me up like a doll and made sure I respected guests and family. I always did everything she told me.

My parents were born in China and are old-fashioned. In the United States, they practice the old customs such as gender preference. In China, most families prefer male to female because males pass on the last name to the next generation. By comparison, females are considered less significant.

My parents focused attention on my oldest brother while I was a shadow in the dark. He got special privileges such as staying out late and doing what he wanted, while I had none. They were busy also with their work.

My mother taught me that males are the dominant ones and females should not go against them. Worst of all, my brother has authority over me. My job in the family is to assist my oldest brother or take care of my younger brothers. I also run errands.

My brother left dirty laundry in the living room. I asked him to pick it up, but he did not listen, so we argued back and forth. My mother came in and told me it is the woman's job to clean the house. I got mad at her for being sexist and stomped out.

I am closer to my mother than my father, but I cannot trust her love because she believes that female is inferior to male in the family. I could not fulfill my mother's desire to be a boy and so I felt betrayed. She punished me for being a girl and caused me to be depressed.

There is little communication with my parents so most of my feelings and thoughts are kept inside. I cannot tell my mother that her belief in female inferiority is wrong because she will not listen. She is too traditional to change her mind about the female role.

My mother worries about how people see her. If we are not well mannered, relatives criticize her for not being a good mother. Concerned with keeping "face," as they called it in China, she put all her time into making sure we behave. But my mother succeeded only through my childhood.

Growling Tiger

As I grew older, I began to disobey my mother in ways that changed my appearance and I did what I wanted instead. One time she got upset with me because I dyed my hair and pierced my ears. She told me that everybody thinks people who dye their hair are bad and wild.

Her source was our conservative relatives who see everything from one point of view. My mother was afraid of what her relatives would think of me, and more important, what they would think of her. So, she insisted I dye my hair black, but I did not listen. Rumors spread that I was out of control.

The rumors became true because my relatives would not allow their daughters to go out with me. This affected me in the sense that I began to see myself as different and bad. I felt guilty when my mother criticized my appearance and I started to believe the rumors were true.

I isolated myself from social gatherings because I was affected by their criticisms. Now, I realize I am not the way they describe me. I am not wild, disobedient or out of control. I have become more mature. Before, I believed others opinions were important and that I must conform to be happy.

But I have learned to be happier and disregard what other people think. My relatives' view is based on appearance and not on the real me. If I think I am good, then I am good. Who I think I am is who I am.

For example, we were in the living room and my mother asked me to go pay bills. "I will pay the bills after the show." From the look on her face, she was surprised. I do not argue with her any more. I know she picks me because I am reliable and not because I am inferior.

Later that day she told me I was growing each day and I smiled. I was happy to know that she noticed the change in me. I do not get jealous any more when my mother gives my brother special treatment and we all argue less.

I know the conflict between my mother and myself is in my mind. I believed I was not as smart, strong and as good as the boy. So, whenever I blame my mother for being sexist, it is really me blaming myself for not being a boy. In changing my mind about myself, the misunderstanding is resolved.

I am as smart, strong and capable but blinded by my idea of being inferior. I betrayed myself in not loving myself to begin with. No one can hurt me unless I believe it. I no longer see myself as a victim of gender preference. Being a female and the middle child is a blessing.

I am as smart, strong and capable but blinded by my idea of being inferior. I betrayed myself in not loving myself to begin with. No one can hurt me unless I believe it. I no longer see myself as a victim of gender preference. Being a female and the middle child is a blessing.

It is positive because I am the center of the family and I have an older brother and sister who I look up to, and two younger brothers who look up to me. I allowed myself to learn new ideas because of my willingness. I am happier than I was before.

My future career plan is to become an elementary school teacher, an occupation I wanted to pursue since I was a little girl. Now that I am learning, perhaps I will be a good teacher. Knowing my self-worth, I will help girls and boys who think they are worthless learn to be proud.

I am a female Asian minority who at first affirmed my limitations because of gender, generational and cultural differences and I resisted the achievement of my potential. But, I learned none of these things are true and have found my way to greater success and happiness.

Mirror of Four Strangers
Paulo Dionisio

Vision
In the depths of my mind stands a door with a strange light seeping through its hinges. As I walk toward the door, a mist forms. My heart thumps and my mind thinks "fear." An aging bronze plaque reads, "Halt! Enter if thou seek thyself, but beware. Once the door opens it will never close again." I hesitate but decide to open it. Suddenly, there is a flash of light and I forget who I am.

I hear a familiar voice, "Enter Paulo Dionisio. Born in the Philippines January 25, 1979, who recently turned 21. Enter if you want to know you." An intimidating voice followed, "Ha! You are no JEDI. You are a BARD, a "Bad Ass Rock Dude." I agree with the four principles but I do not always follow them.

As I enter and open my eyes, I find myself in a dark, mysterious room with a mirror before me. The mirror looks odd because, instead of my reflection, it shows four strangers that look like me. One has a determined look, the other a patient look, the third an intimidating look and the last an inquisitive look. One by one they introduce themselves.

"I am Will" the determined stranger answers. Waiting for the others to speak, a second says, "I am Wait." "I am Hate," the third utters in a powerful tone. The inquisitive one then stares at me, and in a majestic tone states, "I am Ether the Mind Bender." He smiles and says, "It is best to explain us one by one."

WILL AND WAIT

Will begins by telling me how I am willing sometimes and not at other times. He then shows me a movie in the mirror about one of my experiences where my willingness was weak. It was last year, when I wanted to learn to sing. My younger sister tells me to play the guitar because my voice is hopeless. Nevertheless, I took lessons, but did not practice very often.

Still, I improved. I can now sing with a powerful tone in a limited range and only when alone or in front of my voice teacher. I played in a recital to test my new voice. With my guitar strapped on my back, I played and sang my version of the Doors' masterpiece: *People are Strange.*

Though there were technical problems with my voice, people complimented my performance. "This shows even if your willingness to learn is small, you managed to sing well," said Will, as the movie faded to an end. I accept willingness as one of my principles but only in pursuit of what interests me.

It was Wait's turn, but all he did was stare at me. A movie about trying to join or form a band appeared. When I graduated to intermediate guitar player, my only connection to musicians was my teacher. I asked him how to find players around my age to jam with me.

He said that I could post an advertisement on the bulletin board in music stores and schools. I also surfed the Internet and found a bass player. He came over to my apartment and we jammed for hours. That was the first and the last time we played together.

But I played with my high school friends when I was in the Philippines for summer break, my cousin during a family get together and my guitar teacher. On the way home from a lesson, a guy asked if I wanted to jam with him. I agreed and we played Hendrix's *Foxy Lady* and some exhilarating impromptu blues.

We attracted a few people and he asked if I want to be the first member of his band, *Seymour and the Soldiers*. At last, I was in a band. But his landlord kicked him out of his apartment on account of the noise. Someday, I will find the perfect band. As the movie ended, I realized I have been patient.

HATE

I still do not have "consciousness." Sometimes I do, but most times I do not. It was Hate's turn to explain himself. He is an intimidating guy with flaming red hair and an icy stare. He shows me a movie about my senior year in high school back home in the Philippines.

High school there was different. Teachers move from one classroom to another. You have the same classmates in every class until the end of the school year. I did not agree with the social hierarchy in my class. I chose to be an outcast because the elite, cool people were boring.

I had no enemies at first, but later I began to hate the cool people. They tried to use us as stepping-stones. They picked on us and labeled us "autistic." At first, I was proud of the label, but my fellow autistics were not. So, the label became a drag for me too. I felt like a silly clown and berated myself for being one.

I blamed the cool people. Every time they picked on us, I would counter attack with some sarcastic remark. I was called a wild and unpredictable autistic. I still hated them when we graduated. But I was proud to be a unique autistic.

There are times now when I rebuke myself and criticize others. So, the phantom enemy appears and disappears. I agree with the third principle, but Hate is always in the mirror, though I know I see self-hate. He fades but always comes back because I believe he hates me.

ETHER

Ether the Mind Bender tells me not to be afraid or angry at Hate. Hate is sometimes useful for example, in composing and playing punk rock songs. I begin to hear Jimi Hendrix's *Purple Haze* and find myself engulfed in a purple haze of tranquility. "Do not be afraid," Ether speaks with a soothing voice. I compose my own song, *For Shame and For Fame*.

I am not cool enough to play punk rock because I am too clean. I do not take drugs or smoke tobacco. I begin to hate myself for not being cool, but then I turn it around. I will be cool about cool. I write a hybrid tune, with psychedelic, jazz and punk elements. It is raw, loud and weird compared to mainstream music but it is my masterpiece.

At times, Ether is weaker and Hate takes over. Homework and school projects usually make Ether bend. I wrote a research paper for political science and I got a C. I tried to be interested in the topic but had writer's block. Ether tells me that the source of his power is my interest that is filed in Will's department.

I begin to analyze the situation. I agree with the four principles, but I do not always follow them. I am only willing and patient if I am interested in the subject. I am also sometimes angry. I do not follow the light side, nor the dark side of the force. I follow my own side that is often no side.

I am a BARD, not a JEDI. I choose to be one but I cannot always follow the advanced principles. The four strangers in the mirror are strangers to me no more. Their images merge into one crazy person that shatters to a million pieces. Does this mean seven years of good luck?

Suddenly, the shards of the bard from the mirror become silver butterflies. They fly past me and away through the darkness, removing my clothes as they sweep by, leaving me naked and alone. Perhaps I am not insane and can start afresh with self-trust and my creative mind.

Far Away From Home
Qiao (Jo) Kang

Trip Out

There is a friend I have not seen for a long time since she moved to Earth. Our story goes like this: we were best friends when we both lived on a faraway planet called Heaven. A few years later, she left our home and since that time I have never seen her again. I heard she moved to a strange new place. That is how we got separated.

Two weeks ago, luckily, I got in contact with her and made my plan for a visit. My trip to Earth exhausted me and for three long days, I could not wake up. When I awoke, memories flashed in front of my eyes, but could not recall where I came from. All I can see is my Earth friend enthusiastically talking to me.

"My dear enemy, I am glad you came to visit me . . ." Oh, at home we call our friends enemies — remember? You were my best enemy in childhood! This is your first time here, so why not allow me to show you around, how is that?

As I wrote to you, I live in a place of illusion. Everyone here is dressed in fancy clothes and wears nice makeup. The way we are taught, we try to look elegant all the time. Yes, we are vain, but occasionally we hear an inner voice telling us to trust in some "higher power." It bugs me!

But do not worry we are safe here. I am sure nothing can harm us. Besides, we all learn to deny and ignore our true identity anyway. Of course, the most effective way to cope is to pretend — that is right— just pretend you hear no voice at all, and believe instead in Evil. What? How can you not understand what I am saying?

By the way, do you like my new mask and space suit? We were scared when the air quality damaged our skin and lungs. Our great scientists came together and invented outfits for us. They fit perfectly. No one has complained since we started protecting ourselves. Children do not wear the new suits because their faces and bodies are too small.

Peace Poem

Willingness: *I know what I want.*
Patience: *I have faith in the future.*
Phantom Enemy: *I know all my enemies are false.*
Mind Power: *I have no limitations.*

Whitney Arnold

They will wear them when they turn eighteen. Lucky kids! Actually, I still have an extra. Do you want one? No? Some of the Innocents attempted to take off their masks to get fresh air. How dangerous! You know, once I . . . My friend just went on and on. She is quite talkative and makes me speechless. But I have been patient the whole trip.

If you have never heard of Earth let me explain it to you. Earth is in the realm of illusions. It is the exact reverse of our world. There is a supernatural power here called Evil and people are the Innocents. The interrelation among them is simply this: evil controls the whole planet and the Innocents form a system to worship it.

In our realm, we worship others as ourselves because we know we are one. But people here believe illusions are real and see Evil within others. The Innocents are born with a natural ability to push Evil away, but many have decided already to go back home. Yet, all of them will one day leave Earth.

Trip Back

I am incredibly happy now that I know I will be getting back to Heaven. The Innocents are pathetic. I can hardly stand being in this place longer. I pity my friend. Her mask makes her look like someone I do not know. She has no idea how beautiful she is.

Innocents have no idea how their ugly outfits hide their true selves. I worry for my friend — and wish I could help her. But I cannot stay away from home any longer, even in a mask, space suit and the company of a good friend. Once I got back, I sent her this message:

Dear Jo

This is your best enemy from planet Heaven (back home we call friends enemies). I got back safely and the return trip was easier than leaving. Before I left, I imagined you as quite a different girl. I did not expect to see you in a space suit. Jo, you really have changed a lot while you have been gone. You are a stranger to me now. The place where you live is so different from here.

As a friend, I respect the way you are and accept the way I am. I wish I could persuade you to change, though I know it does not matter. The law here says we can invite anyone home but no pressure is allowed. I know you know the way home but have forgotten. Honoring the law, let me just remind you that you are always welcome to come and stay.

This is the only place where people find impossible things like real happiness and peace. So, please, come for a visit and you will soon see what has kept me content here for so long. If you like, you can come through a wormhole in your mind, until you decide to relocate permanently.

Though the distance between us is great in this moment, it feels like you are right here next to me. How wonderful it will be when you come home for good from your journey so far away. Are we still good friends? Can we become best enemies again? I am looking forward to our future together. Your true and original self . . .

Sincerely, Jo

TWELVE

NOVICE: WILLINGNESS

Instead of "quiet desperation," most people want sincerely to lead lives of purpose and fulfillment. The achievement of this goal begins with a simple intention. Principle 1, therefore, is about willingness — the basic act of altering your point of view. Out of wanting to learn, individual consciousness evolves.

Aspiration of any percent is the key — the only key — and is a matter of free choice. You may think willingness means 100% commitment, but this miscalculation interferes with getting started. A commitment of .01% or less, but not zero, works. Without willingness, personal and social change await reception for as long as it may take — a lifetime if necessary — for God is patient.

Drill & Review

Any Percent Willing

Willingness is necessary because there must first be a desire to develop. Aspiration is natural to a wisdom hero who tries to stay mindful of anger and attack in thought and action. Any force used to introduce awareness contradicts consent. It is impossible, therefore, to be bent against your will and pressed into peace service.

A modest invitation initiates the process and with patience, elevates the aspirant to the level of apprentice. Unlike the hero in the 1998 Walt Disney Studios animated film *Mulan*, no one can volunteer in place of another. Based on ancient Chinese legend, the young heroine takes her infirm father's place in the army when barbarian Huns invade their country.

Ready to Learn

Peace knighthood does not ask everything of you but only your willing mind. The power of God lends you strength and makes you immune to all weakness. You cannot be forced to be willing. Enthusiasm is optional and stamina unnecessary. A simple desire signifies readiness to learn and you are hereby self-promoted to the second stage of apprenticeship.

You do not transform yourself; you simply allow change to happen by giving your grateful mind to the process. A sense of moral obligation darkens the spark of light in your thinking. You can choose to remain in the dark or in the light, reactive or reflective, trapped or freed. Resistance makes the goal look unattainable, creates self-doubt, feels awful and impedes lift-off.

Immune from Weakness

To get started you do not need the deep inner knowledge and healing power of the perfect love of the almighty force. Yoda's idea of "deep commitment" and "serious responsibility" are burdensome to a novice. Experience comes with age, but wisdom comes only with the desire for it. Willingness honors the law of faith in a greater power deep within your mind. ("My strength is made perfect in weakness" 2 *Corinthians* 12:9).

"Being responsible" and "accepting the consequences of your actions" make the decision seem arduous and arouses fear about making an "irresponsible" choice. If you make a mistake, however, still you are not guilty though you may think so. Pending the right decision, your development is delayed only because negative thinking intervenes. Even when the choice is wrong, you are being responsible, for at least you want to grow.

Willingness Heads the Soul

Greater responsibility comes after the decision, not before. Making the choice for faith in God, unburdened by guilt about responsibility, liberates you immediately from the "dark side." Willingness is the head of the soul and you have a head start. Once willingness opens your mind to intuitive wisdom, you do not need to be more responsible for thinking or action until you are ready to develop more fully.

To get started you may want help, but no matter how much encouragement you receive, unless you first change your mind, nothing will happen. Then you can claim it does not work for you. Nor will a kick in the posterior overcome the inertia of being unwilling. So, if willingness is not enough, you are still fearful and guilty. There is nothing before willingness except not being willing.

Willingness is the maximum output to begin. You allow yourself to think that the law of faith works within you. It is not absolute but you can be aware only of one self at a time. ("No man can serve two masters" *Matthew* 6:24). Willingness is the proverbial "mustard seed" of faith (*Matthew* 17:20). Because willingness is tiny, wisdom knighthood is for motivationally challenged people of every color, shape and size.

and Gives You a Head Start

The opportunity exists through willingness and not through social opportunities, political action, market promotions, genetic inheritance, good fortune or good fortune cookies. You control "the universe" with mind power. That knighthood happens is a matter of clarity about what you want, moment by moment, not intensity of desire, experience or length of service.

You Parent Yourself

You may be devoted to a higher power after you are willing but not before. Regardless of who your father or mother are, or what either has done to you, parents matter only if they contribute to you parenting your soulful self. Luke would not have become a peace knight had he not been willing. He inspires and illustrates the process. You need no faith, but only willingness to learn to have faith. No mortal has full faith in God.

APPRENTICE: PATIENCE

Being in a hurry reflects inner discord. In stage two, an apprentice practices the art of being relaxed and calm, the tranquil prelude to absorbing Principles 3 and 4 (recognizing the phantom enemy and harnessing the power of the mind). Impatience is but a disguise for not trusting yourself. Without patience, you are engulfed by war and like Brer Rabbit, stuck in a patch of tar, exactly what "the enemy" seeks.

Two Sports of the Ego

You cannot be in a hurry to be patient. There is no risk of getting sidetracked because you are already off-road in a civil war in your mind. Luke creates the diversion he needs — escaping to rescue his friends in trouble. Popular ways of reproducing guilt and getting off-track that can last a lifetime, involve: accidents, injuries, lawsuits, romances, children and illnesses. Fighting and love-making are the two great sports of the ego.

The excitement of both diversions insulates you from self-trust by focusing attention on physical sensation. Patience, however, makes you receptive to incoming Principles 3 and 4. Impatience makes time the enemy, distraction a protection, impulsiveness a lifestyle that block consciousness. Luke acts as though Yoda invented the principle of patience to personally persecute him.

Beginners often gratify the senses and lose patience, wanting to graduate before they matriculate and to skip over developmental stages. They have not yet learned that the source of all knowledge is not books, libraries, laboratories, computers, conferences, teachers and mentors. Courageous perseverance characterizes the fourth stage, but willingness induces the process of change.

A Pin-Ray of Light

As soon as willingness opens your mind, it is on to Principle 2, which involves understanding that spiritual clarity may take time if you need it. If you are impatient, you think that anger is justified and enlightenment difficult. Thus, it may take you yet another lifetime to find peace. If you relax, a pin-ray of light, representing willingness, breaks through the darkness of self-doubt.

Once the light burns, it cannot be snuffed out and patience keeps it steady. Time can never be wasted while learning patience, for what you learn is timelessness. "I'll be patient when I find time," is only true in reverse; you will find time only when you are patient. Things done in a hurry are usually done poorly and rushing worries everyone. "I have been patient too long," is illogical — if you are patient, you remain patient.

"Padawan" is a term for an apprentice of the Force. This is Luke's level in *Empire Strikes Back*, Obi-Wan's in *Phantom Menace* and Anakin's in *Attack Clones*. According to Robert Vitas' *Unofficial Star Wars Encyclopedia*, Padawans are distinguished by close-cropped hairstyles accented by a thin braid. "The braid's length, together with small beads braided into the hair, denotes the Padawan's level of training." The focus on braids and beads indicates that the mind is still knotted and twisted with doubt about the self.

You Learn Timelessness

DISCIPLE: PHANTOM ENEMY

Prisoner of the 'Dark Side'

Once Luke demonstrates willingness and patience, he becomes a novice and then an apprentice. But he is intimidated when Yoda introduces Principles 3 and 4 because he believes the enemy is real and that violence is the only solution. Argue for a shadow-self and it appears like Shakespeare's ghost of Hamlet's father. To exist within the dark side is no real choice in light of the love of God.

Luke thinks Darth Vader is a mass murderer, a ruthless despot, who seeks to obliterate goodness in the galaxy. He believes there are intrinsic evil acts like rape, murder and genocide. Further, the galaxy is full of greed, exploitation and brutality. Consequently, Principle 3, recognizing the phantom enemy, is regarded as a trap set by the naive Yoda instead of the sinister Darth Vader.

As a military man, Luke relies on physical training and muscular stamina to feel powerful. He fears the loss of his meager might if he pays attention to awesome mind power. Luke sees backwards, however, through the filter of the fear of defeat, rather than the crystal of clear victory. The band he leads is tormented precisely to stop his training — to cause him to fight for their release and to shackle him again as prisoner to the "dark side."

Fighter & Lover

Therefore, he breaks training on the pretext that he must save his friends from the clutches of this nasty adversary. At the same time, Han and Leia become enthralled in romantic love. Secretly, Luke fears that the celibacy implied in becoming a wisdom hero will make him impotent, instead of an outstanding man of action. He thinks he must escape Yoda's regimen to preserve being a fighter and lover (Chapter 9).

When biology is destiny, genitals are jewels to be treasured, and peace is regarded as a test of the testes. Luke does not yet understand that the "dark side" is illusory — confronted irrationally by coercion and violence. Carl G. Jung once wrote, "Conflict exists strictly as an opportunity to raise consciousness." ("For there is no power but the power of God" *Romans* 13:1).

Luke falls for Darth Vader's ploy and postpones learning advanced Principles 3 and 4. He reverts to gross measures of control and prevents the arrival of disciple and master status until *Episode VI*. For now, he strikes out and reinforces "evil" in the prevailing illusion of cosmic injustice. Gullibly resuming militant measures, he appears to empower the evil warlord. But never can you conquer a "dark side" that is not there.

Test of the Testes

God is monistic, not dualistic. No "dark side," no opposite, has any substance outside the reality given to it by the imagination. The darkness of evil cannot exist in light of a larger power that is totally good and wholly limitless. Just as there is no night in daylight, shadows exist only where shields are erected to shade the light. When this truth is realized, the devil is deposed as a god in your mind and you are no longer reviled in self-hate.

A disciple starts to trust the love of God. He or she realizes that any conflict with another is always projected self-conflict and an opportunity to heal. The Lords of the Sith are false appearances of the self that have no power because they have no real substance. Evil appears and multiplies only because it embodies the underlying premise that you are guilty. With this new consciousness, the veil of evil is lifted and the peace menace vanishes.

Monistic Not Dualistic

As an apparition, enemies are a category of hateful misperception of the self. While you are unconsciously in the projection, you lack the overall vision to see the illusion. To extricate yourself, you need a frame of reference in the light, to see in the dark, that attacking others always reflects self-hate. You not loving yourself is misconstrued as others not loving you.

A mirror reflects your appearance, not your essence. The "evil" you see in others reveals your own self-misconception, for ugliness and beauty are in the eyes of the beholder. The "enemy" is the self-centered part of your mind that repudiates the unconditional love of God and initiates an attack cycle. But you are guilty only as long as you believe your projections are real. Attacking clones disguise self-hate as "enemies."

Attack Clones = Self-Hate

Conflict is an illusion — anywhere, anytime, always. Your worst enemy is your best friend because he or she reveals exactly where God stands in your mind. It does not follow that your best friend is your worst enemy because the idea of an "enemy" is mistaken, as is the idea that "the enemy of your enemy is your friend." The only way to win a war is not to fight because the opponent is an illusion of self-mistrust arising from being in the wrong mind.

To know there are no enemies is to see you as limitless from the point of view of the whole. Holding a grudge maintains that you are a victim of some limitation. You are confined or liberated by the image you hold of you. You either adore or abhor the spiritual self, but raised in the matrix, you learn to think backwards. You are capable of loving yourself but do not recognize your potential when, like Yoda, it looks so peculiar.

Worst Enemy = Best Friend

To love enemies means to "kill" them with kindness. To prepare a table for thine enemies (*Psalms* 23:5) invites you to be gracious and generous. You do not need to wine and dine adversaries, but be kind and thoughtful to them in your mind. This allows you to receive the gift of love that is yours to have, symbolized in sharing conversation and meals with others. You do not need to fear false gods because they are fake, nor the true God, because God is real.

"Enemies" do to you what they think you have done to them. You are considered guilty of doing to them exactly what they are doing back to you, since they believe you have done it to them first. In their eyes, therefore, you deserve it. They would not attack you, however, if they did not feel guilty of what you are being accused of doing to them. You would not be attacking in return, if you did not believe you were also guilty and deserving of attack.

God is Real

The "logic" of anger and attack is convoluted. Others mirror the self, always and exactly, representing the mislocated you. Projections go back and forth, and conflicts go round and round, until one party realizes that neither is guilty and withdraws. In all disputes, both sides are holy even while believing the other is a spiteful foe. In *A New Hope*, however, Luke thinks mind power involves denying evil when it really is there.

Darth Vader is a phantom enemy defeated by the realization that he exists only hypothetically. Evil comes to be regarded as a category of mistaken perception about the "reality" of a dark side and the "unreality" of God. Mindful of Principles 3 and 4, Luke sees the good in his father and saves humanity by surrendering in the war with God. Darth Vader sees himself in the eyes of his loving son who redeems him at the end of two trilogies.

Phantom enemy means the enemy in "reality" is imaginary. It does not mean there is an enemy you do not see. To follow your destiny you do not need to stop fighting the devil, but only to recognize that you also unconsciously fight God mentally. You allow the clandestine peace knight to rise to consciousness and openly represent you as an ally in daily life. God loves unconditionally and forgives even when he is "betrayed" by a lack of awareness.

Enemies are Imaginary

As peace hero, Luke Skywalker detaches from "the world" of violence and vengeance. Like Luke, almost everyone rejects this idea at first because it asserts that the "dark side" reflects the shadows of doubt about your place in eternal sunlight. The premise begins to sink in, however, with the acquisition of inner peace as an outcome of willingness and patience, when the prescience (foreknowledge) of God is felt.

Love & Forgive

Thich Nhat Hanh, a Vietnamese Buddhist monk, nominated for the Nobel Peace Prize by Martin Luther King in 1967, in *Touching Peace* (1992) wrote, "We do not have to die to enter the kingdom of heaven." A tranquil option exists in every tormented clash and radiates its healing light through us to others. This is the "peace of God which surpasseth all understanding" (*Philippians* 4:7).

MASTER: MIND POWER

Once Luke's accomplices are freed by the midpoint of *Return of the Jedi*, he returns to training with Yoda but finds the little sage on his deathbed. Altruistically, Yoda knows he must expire for Luke to realize that the Force is his possession. Yoda reminds Luke to confront Darth Vader (in his mind) and demonstrates the immortality of Jedi Knights by passing to the spiritual plane.

Through his mentor's decision, Luke at last comprehends that lesson four is about confronting "Darth Vader" psychologically. Now ready for promotion to master, Luke uses the power of his mind to bring an end to the wars of *Star Wars*. When he sees the basic good in his spiritual father, Anakin Skywalker, at the core of his biological father, Darth Vader, he throws away his light saber — an incredible act for a fighter.

Mind Power Master

Luke recognizes that there is no enemy and that evil does not exist anywhere in the galaxy. With the acceptance of mind power, Luke promotes himself to the rank of full-fledged Jedi Knight and unites with the Force. This allows him to see goodness in his father, too, who now is someone to redeem rather than condemn. Seeing the re-release of *Return of the Jedi*, a ten-year old boy reportedly told his mother, "Darth Vader was saved because Luke loved him so much" (and vice versa).

Darth Vader recognizes his own basic goodness and demotes the awful emperor by throwing him into the abyss of material reality where his dark energy explodes into the nothingness it always is. You "overthrow" the enemy by dismissing the validity of the idea in your mind. Father and child surrender to the Light and turn in their "weapons" — the fierce emperor for the father and the little light saber for the son.

No Enemy Anywhere

Though Darth Vader is an archetype of the devil, Luke removes his father's (hardheaded) helmet and deceptive mask, upon request, to reveal his true self and therefore, he resumes the form of Anakin Skywalker, his pre-satanic identity. "You already have [saved me] Luke. You were right. You were right about me. Tell your sister . . . you were right." If the "devil" can be saved, then no dualism of good and bad can exist.

Darth Vader is transformed back into Anakin Skywalker and his name and identity change back and forth because his consciousness changes. In the light of faith, Darth Vader does not exist. The spirit of serenity reigns supreme as the trinity of Yoda, Obi-Wan and Anakin beam radiantly from their perch in eternity. Peace is lasting — no longer just a break in galactic combat.

Initially, people *are* afraid of the Light and *are not* afraid of the dark. As the psychological component of "sin," guilt seems real. Darkness can be seen with the eyes, but light is all that prevails beyond the veil. Denial ends when you realize that you are afraid to join the peace band because you are its conductor. Fearing failure, you stay angry to avoid risking faith, continuing self-attacks of guilt and blaming others to hide the war with God.

Throws Away Weapon

From: jafaculty@hotmail.com
Sent: Monday, January 06, 2003
To: jsnodgr@calstatela.edu
Subject: Peace Knight Path

Peace Knight Path

Your book is a different look at *Star Wars* than I have ever read and I must say, thought provoking and refreshing. I honestly never made the connections you drew from the films. I do not relate to the "psychobabble," but it does not interfere with your main points that are superb and very much in accord with what we teach at the Jedi Acad-emy. It is a finely crafted work and compelling. It made me contemplate my own path and how to be a "Jedi" in real life.

Alcander Caedmon
Jedi Academy Faculty

Vaya Con La Fuerza

Spiritual mind power is kept conscious or unconscious with the intention of the mind, but it is always there whether you realize it or not. Forgiveness reveals that enemies are phantoms — illusions about who we think we are before we assume our divine identity. When the One Mind fills in the one mind, the domain of indi-vidual and Universal coincides. "May the Force be with you," then is a decision that you make.

Thirteen

Right of Passage

Peace knights are keepers of the wisdom that humanity is raised from lower consciousness, based on the senses, to higher consciousness, based on the pensive mind. Luke Skywalker begins to acquire this understanding as a young man who leaves childhood behind to embark on the heroic journey to faith. "Knighthood" is equivalent to "adulthood" and *Star Wars* is a coming-of-age story with which everyone can identify.

For Luke, the struggle involves Obi-Wan Kenobi, his spiritual father, contra Darth Vader, his biological father. He must make a choice as to whom he pledges allegiance. One option is to be like his genetic father, who he resembles in appearance, and to rebel or conform, in a world of forms. His ambition is to be bigger and stronger since he always has been smaller than his father. To excel by any other means is unimaginable to a child.

Identity & Destiny

Genetic or Spiritual Parents?

From birth to adulthood (0-21) children acquire an identity based on anatomy and the mind-body connection is deeply implanted in their psyche. In the second half of the lifespan (21+) conceptual thinking makes possible a choice. Instead of conformity or rebellion, there is the option of maturation. That is, you may resemble your biological parents outwardly but learn to think like your Mother-Father inwardly.

Typically, the choice is faced during the midlife crisis in middle adulthood (28-49). The ego is then challenged by physiological deterioration and failures in social life. The crucial age is thirty-five for women and forty for men. No one has to wait this long, nor be traumatized, however, before deciding to mature. In a rupture of a different kind in recent years, some people have awakened to a totally loving light through near death experiences.

You can become autonomous — exercise a third option — and think in line with Spiritual Parents whom you resemble in abstract form. This is a quantum jump in consciousness; just as becoming a grown man or woman are leaps beyond childhood in reproductive capacity. People tend to think, however, that spiritual growth occurs by default when you are too old to fight and win — when aging inevitably resigns you to death.

Adults Grow Mentally & Mature Inwardly

In getting older, the immature mind sees only awful decay — the persistence of a natural perspective. Unlike wine, humans are not considered to improve with vintage. An alternative to being self-centered, however, is to trust that appearance means nothing in life and death. Your right mind can deliver you from your wrong mind. In thinking you decompose and grow ugly, you can go to peace, instead of pieces.

People tend to remember their spiritual potential while in despair and to forget when they recover from a painful ordeal. But you terrorize yourself unmercifully in life all the time by depending on youth and beauty in a perishable body as the source of identity and destiny. As the naked eye sees only the surface, getting older makes the underlying guilt about being frail seem real. Grown-ups, however, learn not to tell time.

Maturity is Mental and Optional

The search for the meaning of life challenges everyone in every generation in the journey through linear time and three-dimensional space. Like the changing of the seasons and the spinning of the planet, you can grow up to find the truth beyond the ego-body. Maturity is mental, but optional in adulthood. You give up impulsive thinking, in exchange for wisdom, in an inner life cycle.

Most people on the surface of the planet, however, are in preconscious states of mind. "It's worth remembering," wrote Colin McGinn (2002) that *matrix* originally meant *womb* — so that humans are in effect prenatal dreamers." *A Course in Miracles* advises, "being awake within the dream" or "being in the world but not of it." Still, your ego thinks you are a swell person. With faith, however, the ego is deflated.

The decision to awaken cannot be done without your consent, nor by another, but it can be postponed. Because the ego is arrogant, aspirants to faith want a guide — a selfless, older, wiser guru like Yoda. Without willingness, however, the thought that you are born in sin and bathed in guilt retards mind power. This handicap can be overcome, just as you can give up wanting to join, or rebel, against parents, teachers and society.

Inner Life Cycle

To facilitate the transformation and to establish the precedence of peace, Luke is inducted into the secret teachings of an ancient mystery religion known as the Jedi Knights of the Force. Do you take Darth Vader or Anakin Skywalker to be your faithfully bound parent? Like Luke, the only battle that exists in the galaxy is the one with God hidden in your mind over life and death. All humanity is terminally ill.

History is History

As the first of a new breed, Luke escapes the prison of self-persecution to save himself and the universe from confinement to the body. As he matures in time and space, history becomes history and the past is bygone — no matter who his parents were — nor what was done to him in earlier times. You are never alone or forgotten when you remember the love of God.

No power in the universe (of the mind) can hold back awakened consciousness, or as French author and social critic Victor Hugo (1802-1885) wrote, "No army can withstand the might of an idea whose time has come." Light is always faster than dark, which has no speed at all. When wanting to be special no longer excites the ego and arouses the body, humans fulfill the inscription on the tomb of King Arthur — "The once and future king."

REMEMBRANCE

At first, Luke thinks he has enemies because he believes he is fragile instead of invincible with mind power. He therefore seeks military training in an elite warrior caste to defeat the cruel commander of death who is but an imaginary part of his own projected self-hate. Luke possesses the fidelity of peace knights, but distracted by wanting to be bigger and stronger than his father, he preconceives a way to victory.

Powered by Mind

Luke's combative methods imitate his father as a fallen angel, and at first, Luke is corrupted in his thinking. This contributes to losing the galactic war and delaying maturation. But his intellect opens to a tradition of esoteric wisdom: no enemies exist in his mind nor in reality. On the threshold of knowledge, pending the relinquishment of illusions, he lapses in consciousness and defects to the "dark side." He remains self-centered in the body rather than spirit-centered in the Force.

Relinquishing self-attacks refers to a decision of the mind, not to overt action in human relations. If reality is an illusion of pure projection, then no behavior, social or anti-social, has any meaning. Disciplining children and practicing terrorism often arise from love, it is claimed. But assaulting anyone, for any reason, denies God's presence in your mind. We continue to provoke enemies in the perpetual war for non-existing peace (Vidal 2002).

War Shows No Faith

Rude and mean people are never enemies because identity is defined from within rather than from the opinions and actions of others. Only purpose — of the mind and not of conduct — makes any act intrinsically good or bad. This means the new world exists in spiritual vision, not in material form. Peace consciousness is a conception of the self, not an ethical code of conduct. Peace is a craft of the mind, for there is no outer globe to transform.

Adversaries are misperceptions of the self, arising from a belief in the abandonment by God. Attacking others for being "evil" substantiates "evil" and replicates what you want to repudiate. As an effect of thinking, fighting for peace and justice, even against tyrants and terrorists, only perpetuates a cycle of violence.

Fighting follows Newton's first law of physics: for every attack there is a counter attack. Attack and fear beget attack and fear unto the nth generation. That enemies are of the same mind is what the Holy Bible means when it says, "A man's foes shall be they of his own household" *(Matthew 10:36).*

Self-Attacks Project 'Enemies'

The concept that "reality is an illusion" is not the same idea as historical revisionists who claim the non-existence of atrocities like the holocaust in Germany or slavery in the United States. To

No Peace Through Violence

argue that it did not happen, essentially is the same as to argue that it did happen, for neither is true. These two camps dispute which reality is "the reality," but not the reality question. Both views are based on the assumption that the separation from God has actually taken place.

A similar fallacy exists in the theories of the naturalist Charles Darwin and the economist Karl Marx. The idea that "violence is the midwife-locomotive of history," imparts an imperative to time. But the excitement in being destructive is also just fantasy. Violence is useful only as long as "sin" is projected onto others as justification for their being judged inferior and deserving of aggression, enslavement and extermination.

Politics Declines Insight

The task is not to take psychology into politics that exists only by the denial of insight, but to enter into a state of mind that ends *realpolitik* through inner peace. Manipulating human relations causes separated minds to intensify outer conflict. As an ideological stance that believes violence has real meaning, being anti-war is not a peaceful solution. Support or opposition to war appears to reproduce antagonism between "pacifistic-idealists" and "realistic-advocates" of war. A clash of two illusions, however, means absolutely nothing.

Trying to restructure the polarized world of separation is futile. Wanting to change "reality" preserves personal guilt by reinforcing the myth of a "dark side" and making death seem frightful. The fear then is blamed on outsiders, who appear to want to attack to protect also against their own hateful self-attacks. To believe that my guilt justifies assaulting you is irrational. A *Course in Miracles* (ACIM) states, "Therefore, seek not to change the world, but choose to change your mind about the world" and about yourself.

REALPOLITIK: POLITICS BASED ON MIGHT RATHER THAN ETHICS.

The basic conflict is the secret war with God over aging and dying. As a separated body-ego, unconscious guilt makes biological death appear frightful as the ultimate punishment. In the interim, there are many penalties like interpersonal incompatibilities, family alienation, ill health and complimentary depression. All political views are out of touch with the reality of God, however and history is one mass psychosis. Only God-consciousness can bring forth sanity in human relations.

One Mass Psychosis

"May the Force be with you" is a plea to awaken, equivalent to, "Give us this day our daily bread" (*Matthew* 6:11). Being saturated in guilt and fried in fear, believing "evil" is real, in ourselves or in others, can be replaced by the sustenance of peace of mind. "Open thy eyes and thou shall be satisfied with bread" (*Proverbs* 20:13). As a devotional prayer, "Daily Bread" is delicious during all our hungry days and restless nights spinning on the big colored marble in space.

I am an Indivisible!

Remembering the origin of your identity and destiny in the divine world, "anamnesis," is the opposite of "amnesia," started by the big bang of the birth trauma. In the journey through the world of darkness, there are many diversions, but only one real choice, for or against the truth in inner vision. "Individual" is from the Latin meaning "without division." Being "indivisible" is the only way six billion body-egos on the planet are special.

Dual-Minded is Duel Minded

With peace consciousness you join your mind to God and are lifted out of self-absorption as a beast trapped in a degrading body and raised to the dignity of a light being. The shared knowledge of Oneness ends the need for arms and armor, but not for *amour*. Then peace extends through you to others from a Source beyond time and space. If you remain dual-minded, however, you stay duel-minded: gunning for others, divided by guilty self-attacks and separated in a world at war with evil.

Neo
=
The New One

You cannot control your mind believing that you are a physical being because it arouses "the beast" in you who is afraid to die. A decision to stay God-conscious, however, is referred to in the Holy Bible as, "He who has eyes to see and ears to hear." *ACIM* says that denial is a decision not to know. You make the decision to forget and then forget that you make the decision. In the wrong state of mind, however, you still have a choice.

According to *ACIM*, you are asleep in a dream in which you have forgotten that you are the cause of your own experience and play all the characters. An awakening within the mind occurs as an abstract change that shows up as "reality" to accommodate the new point of view. The idea that "perception is projection" confers on you the role of hero (saviour) because you assume responsibility as the dreamer of the dream, for the illusion of the world.

This idea is analogous to Neo dreaming his dream within *The Matrix*. At first, he thinks he battles a malicious conspiracy outside his mind. But when Trinity is incapacitated and he is blinded, he relies on faith to stop Agent Smith. *ACIM* directs you to the kingdom of hell or heaven within your thinking. Neo's incredible abilities mirror your own splendid potential, unfettered by politics and personality. As with Prot in *K-PAX*, the saviour's identity exists in the mind.

P
=
P

In *Signs* (Buena Vista 2002) the hero is a farmer (Mel Gibson) who gives up faith in God, like many people, angry about life's brutality. When his wife is killed in an automobile accident, as metaphor, an alien invasion takes over the planet of his mind. Her body is severed in the same way that she is abruptly taken from him — the way we are all sliced-off from heaven on earth. But the invasion recedes and faith is restored when he witnesses that his children survive his toxic thinking and retain the option of faith, by his example, to endure life's hardships.

Beyond pairs of opposites like "life and death," "good and evil," "man and woman," "mother and father," past all words, categories and archetypes, is God. At the deepest level of discourse, our most profound understanding is that distinction itself, beginning with the thought of radical separation, is the cause of all human suffering. You are bound to the body by psychic pain, not bound to psychic pain by the body. Never can you be a victim while you have the option for faith.

Congenital or Metaphysical

All human suffering derives from not staying aware of Oneness. The fall of our natural parents into distress and misfortune is righted by the resurrection of spiritual parents within the mind. The spirit arises out of the ashes of the physical man or woman and your primal-sensual nature "dies." This is the meaning of the sacrifice of animals in religious ceremonies. It resurrects a spiritual-self from the crucifixion by the ego in the practice of physical habits as a means to salvation.

In the mystery of your being, who do you consider to be your parents? Is it God and Holy Sophia abstractly, or your genetic parents organically? If your father's name is "Joseph" and your mother's name is the "Virgin Mary," who are your real parents? Was Jesus the literal offspring of Joseph and Mary? Did he have real brothers and sisters? "Conception" refers both birth and to thinking, so is your origin congenital or metaphysical?

Just a Big Question?

Ultimately, do you think you exist within or beyond time and space? Is there a God or do you believe there is just this big question? Do you doubt what you believe and then believe what you doubt? Do you say, "In the beginning was the ovum and thesperm?" One day, science will prove that "the Fall" coincides with the big bang that blew us apart from one another at birth on earth. Was there nothing, or was God there, before the big bang beginning began?

Only God creates *ex nihilo* — something out of nothing. The question refers to the beginning of all time and to your individual time in transit on the planet. The answer you formulate creates the kind of world you encounter, because what you are looking for, responds to the consciousness with which you are looking. "I was created as the thing I seek," says *ACIM*. "Reality" is created by your thoughts — so what creates your thoughts — catastrophe or serenity?

No Dark Side

ONE FORCE

Star Wars was written about an advanced technological civilization looking back on its past. This society exists, therefore, in a future not far from our own time. Luke Skywalker's achievement of consciousness reflects humanity's potential in the near century and nuclear moment. Until he becomes a gentle peace giant, however, Luke believes fighting is the answer and he repudiates the Force, replicates the war and repeats the weary history of the world.

"May the wind be against your back" is an ancient mariner's salutation resembling the Christians who say, "May the Lord be with you (and also with you.") Knights of the Jedi say, "May the Force be with you." Jews say *shalom*, Hindus say *shanti* and Muslims say *assalmu alaykum* (peace be with you). Human discretion there may be about God, but there is no equivocation in His love, which never reneges like the weather and people.

In distemper, God did not cast humans apart from paradise and the lessons of peace are contradicted whenever He is portrayed as having a "dark side." He appears to be extinguished only when theLight in your mind is dimmed by doubt. God cannot be divid-ed or ex-cluded, but a peace knight can be mistaken by having a dual identity. Neither can God be out of balance but an individual can be off his or her rocker in choosing the wrong side.

Dimmed by Doubt

IDENTITY & DESTINY

Fair winds and perfect light, cast high in the sky, are provisions for the turbulent trip through territorial time. To be among peace astronauts depends simply on a decision to join hands with the mighty three: Yoda, Obi-Wan and Anakin. A circle is the image of the Self and God, center and circumference, point and whole, because there is no demarcation between exclusion and inclusion.

God is the Self

You are there and always have been there, a member in good standing, tall in the perfect circle where no differentiation into inner and outer spheres exists. In your right-mind no separation into form and no form of separation, is at all possible. That God resides in your mortal mind is the reason the sides of your head are called "temples." You can keep conscious whatever you decide to keep conscious and because of mind power, you are free.

The line where God is with you, and you are with God, is dissolved because there never was a disjunction between you two. He is always with you because She is within you (Chapter 4). The answer lies inside the lines because there is no line between inside and outside. There is only one undifferentiated Self, circumscribed in faith and peace. To trust in God is the one immutable law in life — *"let nothing be done through strife" (Philippians 2:3).*

Becoming a "Justly Evolving and Developing Individual," a JEDI, instead of a SITH, "Suffering Individual Through Hatred," is made possible by allowing the truth to be credible. Difficulty and complexity are convolutions of the ego, though your genius may go undetected. "May the Force be with you" means you have the power of good in to overcome every adversity and adversary. Meanwhile, fighting with others is killing you.

Peace of Mind

The spectacular special effects of *Star Wars* perhaps cloud its brilliant message, but its appeal to everyone at some level is the revela-

The End of War

tion of their own hidden divinity. It is not the force of the will, but the will of the Force that counts. As reliable as the knight (and the day) you are as powerful as the Self you recognize. *Islam* translates as "submission to Allah" — ending the wars of the world — new to all history and even to mythology.

Peace consciousness is a goal worth seeking and you are a worthy monarch with the power of God in your mind. If you are looking for a variety of the religious experience, however, thinking there is some baptismal ceremony, organizational legacy or transcendental ecstasy, then you doubt that peace is simply yours, to have and to hold, until to eternity do you depart, always a peace knight.

Wisdom Test

INSTRUCTIONS

There are many tests of science fiction trivia but here is a set of questions about intuitive wisdom. Take this test before and after reading this book to measure your progress in understanding. The correct answers are based on the principles of human development presented in the text and not on knowledge about the world. Answer True or False by checking the appropriate box.

T F

☐ ☐ 1. To qualify as a wisdom hero you must possess a special precious metal known as "jedite."
☐ ☐ 2. God is with you when you have the right DNA.
☐ ☐ 3. A wisdom hero must be a technological genius in preschool.
☐ ☐ 4. You prove to an elder council that you deserve to be a wisdom hero.
☐ ☐ 5. Only boys and men can be wisdom heroes.
☐ ☐ 6. Anyone can be a wisdom hero and in fact everyone already is one.
☐ ☐ 7. A wisdom hero escapes reality to an imaginary world of fantasy.
☐ ☐ 8. When you trust in mind power, the real world changes.
☐ ☐ 9. The insight of mentors is usually false, arising from the influence of mind altering drugs.
☐ ☐ 10. You need only a little will power to start to become a wisdom hero.
☐ ☐ 11. The idea of personal disgrace is a central concern to wisdom heroes.
☐ ☐ 12. A wisdom hero must be committed absolutely to their mission.
☐ ☐ 13. Once you enter the "dark side," forever does it dominate your destiny.
☐ ☐ 14. You must solve all personal problems before becoming a wisdom hero who solves social problems.
☐ ☐ 15. Peace of mind is important to a wisdom hero as preparation for battle.
☐ ☐ 16. The phantom enemy means there is an enemy you do not see.
☐ ☐ 17. You act like a wisdom hero whether you believe it or not.
☐ ☐ 18. Wisdom heroes swear to fight the phantom enemy with all their might.
☐ ☐ 19. The phantom enemy usually starts the fight with a wisdom hero first.
☐ ☐ 20. The phantom enemy is the enemy that does not exist.
☐ ☐ 21. The mind projects the phantom enemy due to not understanding that the enemy is oneself.

☐ ☐ 22. The power of the mind is also known as "the Force."
☐ ☐ 23. Writing poetry is one way of researching inner space.
☐ ☐ 24. One meaning of "light saber" is "to know the light."
☐ ☐ 25. When willing, you find a teacher, and when patient, you find a student of your own.
☐ ☐ 26. Being a wisdom hero opens your mind to an energy source in the galaxy.
☐ ☐ 27. Wisdom heroes cannot eliminate evil in the world but prevent these forces from taking over.
☐ ☐ 28. Wisdom heroes learn to control others' minds and to levitate physical objects.
☐ ☐ 29. You must take vows of poverty and chastity to be a wisdom hero.
☐ ☐ 30. If you were totally logical you would not resist being a wisdom hero.

Wisdom Level

Novice	Apprentice	Disciple	Master
(0-7)	(8-14)	(15-21)	(22-30)
⇨	⇨	⇨	⇨

(number correct)

Answer Key
1. F 6. T 11. F 16. F 21. F 26. F
2. F 7. F 12. F 17. T 22. T 27. F
3. F 8. F 13. F 18. F 23. T 28. F
4. F 9. F 14. F 19. F 24. T 29. F
5. T 10. T 15. F 20. T 25. T 30. T

CANON OF STAR WARS

The "canon" of *Star Wars* is not a starship weapon. From biblical studies, "canon" refers to materials considered "orthodox" by experts. A debate means there is no agreement about a singular creator of the *Star Wars* universe. George Lucas is author and director of *A New Hope*, including the screenplay, novel and film. But under authorization, others directed the next two episodes and wrote the novels and screenplays.

Lucas drafted both trilogies, the screenplay of *Episode I, IV* and is coauthor of *Episode VI*. Leigh Brackett and Lawrence Kasdan are cited as authors of *Return of the Jedi*. Lucas is also the executive producer of both the prequel, the sequel and the Special Edition film series. But the canon is not fixed and any definition is arbitrary.

Canon in this book was considered to be: the film scripts (including early drafts) of the five films, the five novels and the three revised films of the Special Edition. The *Star Wars Radio Drama* falls into this category but the twelve episodes were not consulted (available on the Internet and on DVD). This definition of "the bible" excludes voluminous licensed, as well as, unlicensed materials.

The three classic novels are available in one edition as *The Star Wars Trilogy* (New York: Ballantine Books, 1993). The first novel was credited to George Lucas but reportedly ghostwritten by Alan Dean Foster. The second and third novels were authorized by Lucas and written respectively by Donald F. Glut and by James Kahn. Terry Brooks penned the novel of *Phantom Menace*. R.A. Salvatore is the novelist of *Star Wars: Episode II: Attack of the Clones*.

Several biographies appeared in 1999. The most detailed was by John Baxter, *Mythmaker: The Life and Work of George Lucas* (New York: Avon Books, 1999). Sally Kline edited a collection of interviews: *George Lucas: Interviews* (Jackson, MS: University of Mississippi Press, 1999). Two books discuss *Star Wars* using the theories of Carl G. Jung: Steven A. Galipeau, *Journey of Luke Skywalker: An Analysis of Modern Myth and Symbol* (Chicago: Open Court Publishers, 2001) and Susan Mackey-Kallis, *The Hero and the Perennial Journey Home in American Film* (Philadelphia: University of Pennsylvania Press, 2001).

A rare philosophical analyses of *Star Wars* is an article written by Matthew C. Mohs, untitled and undated (mds.mdh.se/~uks/starwars/article/paper.txt). A second is the companion volume to the 1997-1998 Smithsonian Institution exhibition: Mary Henderson, *Star Wars: The Magic of Myth* (New York: Bantam Doubleday Dell Publishers, 1997).

Three recent books with *Star Wars* in the title are: Shelly Durrell, *Healing the Fisher King: Spiritual Lessons with Parzival, Gump, the Grail, Tao and Star Wars* (Miami FL: Art Tao Press, 2002); Michael J. Hanson and Max S. Kay, *Star Wars: The New Myth* (Philadelphia, PA: Xlibris Corp, 2002); and John Porter, *The Tao of Star Wars* (Humanics Publishing Group, 2003).

On the Internet there are 1,500 non-official *Star Wars* websites. There are official sites devoted to the Special Edition and all the Prequels (starwars.com). A privately maintained, now defunct, *Frequently Asked Questions List* (FAQ-L) discussed *Star Wars* phenomena with an emphasis on technical issues. Also see Peter J. Weber, *The Incredible Internet Guide to Star Wars* (Tempe, AZ: Facts on Demand Press, 1999).

"The 'Star Wars' Religion" is designed and maintained by Eli Williamson Jones (firesofcreation.net/starwars). A 1998 graduate of Hampshire College, Amherst, Massachusetts, Eli(jah) is a digital artist and screen writer. His homepage was inspired by a college assignment and shows Luke Skywalker confronting Darth Vader. A caption reads, "The Star Wars Trilogy is like a religion that teaches great wisdom about the nature of our lives in this vast universe."

BIBLIOGRAPHY

A Course in Miracles (ACIM). (Glen Ellen, CA: Foundation for Inner Peace, 1992).

Allnutt, Frank. *The Force of Star Wars,* (Old Tappan, N.J.: Spire Books, 1977).

Allnutt, Frank. *Unlocking the Mystery of the Force* (Denver, CO: Allnutt Publishing Co.,1999.

Andreadis, Athena. *To Seek out New Life: The Biology of Star Trek* (New York: Three Rivers Press, 1999).

Amis, Robin. *A Different Christianity: Early Christian Esotericism and Modern Thought* (New York: State University of New York Press, 1995).

Barad, Judy. *The Ethics of Star Trek* (San Francisco: Harper Collins, 2000).

Barrett, Michèle and Barrett, Duncan. *Star Trek: The Human Frontier* (New York: Routledge, 2001).

Baxter, John. *Mythmaker: The Life and Work of George Lucas* (New York: Avon Books, Inc., 1999).

Bergesen, Albert J. and Andrew M. Greeley. *God in the Movies* (New Bruswick: N.J., Transaction Publishers, 2000.

Blades, Kevin. "What About Midichlorians," Star Warz Legacy Website (starwarz.com).

Bouzereau Laurent (editor). *Star Wars: The Annotated Screenplays* (New York: Ballantine Books, 1997).

Bouzereau Laurent and Duncan, Jody. *Star Wars: The Making of Episode I* (New York: Ballantine Publishing Group,1999).

Brooks, Terry. *Star Wars: Episode I: Phantom Menace* (New York: Ballantine Publishing Group, 1999).

Cavelos, Jeanne. *The Science of Star Wars* (New York: St. Martins Press, 1999).

Campbell, Joseph,. *The Hero with a Thousand Faces* (New York: Pantheon Books, Inc. 1949).

Champlin, Charles. *George Lucas: The Creative Impulse: Lucasfilm's First Twenty Five Years* (New York: Harry N. Abrahams, Inc. Publ., 1997).

Chopra, Deepak. *The Way of the Wizard: Twenty Spiritual Lessons for Creating the Life You Want* (NewYork: Random House, 1995).

Cruz, San Juan. Translated and edited by E. Allison Peers, *Dark Night of the Soul* (NewYork: Doubleday, 1959).

Cruz, Sor Juana Inés de la. Translated by Margaret Sayers Peden, *Poems, Protest and Dreams: Selected Writings* (New York: Penguin Books, 1997).

Durrell, Shelly. *Healing the Fisher King: Spiritual Lessons with Parzival, Gump, the Grail, Tao and Star Wars* (Miami FL: Art Tao Press, 2002).

Edwards, Ted. *The Unauthorized Star Wars Compendium: The Complete Guide to the Movies, Comic Books, Novels and More* (New York: Little Brown and Co., 1999).

Flannery-Daily, Frances and Rachel Wagner. *Wake Up! Gnosticism and Buddhism in the Matrix* (whatisthematrix.warnerbros.com) 2002.

Frank, Anne. *Diary of a Young Girl* (New York: Bantam Books, 1993).

Galipeau, Steven A. *Journey of Luke Skywalker: An Analysis of Modern Myth and Symbol* (Chicago: Open Court Publishers, 2001).

Guiness, Alec. *A Positively Final Appearance* (New York: Viking Press, 1999).

Gordon, Andrew. "Star Wars: A Myth for Our Time," edited by Joel W. Martin and Greenwald, Jeff. *Future Perfect: How Star Trek Conquered Planet Earth* (New York: Penguin Putnam Viking, 1998).

Gressh, Lois H. and Weinberg, Robert. *The Computers of Star Trek* (New York: Basic Books, 1999).

Haber, Karen. *Exploring the Matrix: Visions of the Cyber Future* (New York: St. Martin's Press, 2003).

Hanh, Thich Nhat. *Touching Peace: Practicing the Art of Mindful Living* (Parallax Press: Berkeley, CA, 1992).

Hanley, Richard. *Is Data Human: Or, The Metaphysics of 'Star Trek'* (New York: Basic Books, 1998).

Hanson, Michael J. and Max S. Kay. *Star Wars: The New Myth* (Philadelphia, PA: Xlibris Corp, 2002).

Harrison, Taylor. *Enterprise Zones: Critical Positions on Star Trek* (Boulder, CO: Westview Press, 1996).

Henderson, Mary. *Star Wars: The Magic of Myth* (New York: Bantam Doubleday Dell Publisher, 1997).

Horsley, Jake. *Matrix Warrior: Being the One* (London: Gollancz Orion Publishing Group, 2003).

Irwin, William. *The Matrix and Philosophy: Welcome to the Desert of the Real* (Chicago, IL: Open Court Publishing, 2002).

Jenkins, Garry. *Empire Building: The Remarkable Real Life Story of Star Wars* (Seacacus, N.J.: Citadel Press, 1997).

Kline, Sally. Editor, *George Lucas: Interviews* (Jackson, MS: University of Mississippi Press, 1999).

King, Karen L. *The Gospel of Mary of Magdala: Jesus and the First Woman Apolstle* (Santa Rosa, CA: Polebridge Press, 2003).

Knight, Chris. "Midi-chlorians, Physiology, Physics and the Force (theforce.net).

Kraemer, Ross Shephard, William Cassidy and Susan Schwartz. *Religions of 'Star Trek'* (Boulder CO: Westview Press, 2001).

Krauss, Lawrence M. and Stephen Hawking. *The Physics of 'Star Trek.'* (New York: Harper, 1996).

Larsen, Stephen and Robin. *A Fire in the Mind: The Life of Joseph Campbell* (New York:Doubleday), 1991.

Leeper, Mark R. "What's So Good about *Star Wars?*" (reviews.imdb.com) 1987.

Lawrence, John Shelton and Robert Jewett. *The Myth of the American Superhero* (Grand Rapids, MI: William B. Eerdmans Publishing Compancy) 2002.

Mackey-Kallis, Susan. *The Hero and the Perennial Journey Home in American Film* (Philadelphia: University of Pennsylvania Press, 2001).

Marinaccio, Dave. *All I really Need to Know I learned from Watching Star Trek* (New York: Crown Books) 1994.

Maxford, Howard. *The George Lucas Companion: The Complete Guide to Hollywood's Most Influential Film Maker* (London: Batsford B.T., Ltd) 1999).

McGinn, Colin. *The Matrix of Dreams* (whatisthematrix.warnerbros.com) 2002.

Mitchell, Edgar. *The Way of the Explorer: An Apollo Astronaut's Journey Through the Material and Mystical Worlds* (New York: Putnam Publishing Group, 1996).

Mohs, Matthew C. Untitled Article, Undated. (mds.mdh.se/~uks/starwars/article/paper.txt).

Moyers Bill. "Of Myth and Men" (Interview with George Lucas' Theology of *Star Wars*) *Time Magazine* (Apr 26,1999) pp. 90-94.

Nord, Kevin M. "Star Wars Irresistible Force," (swa.simplenet.com).

Ostwalt Jr., Conrad E. *Screening the Sacred: Religion, Myth and Ideology in Popular American Film* (Boulder: CO Westview Press, 1995) pp. 73-82.

Pollock, Dale. *Skywalking: The Life and Films of George Lucas* (Hollywood, CA: Samuel French) 1990.

Pounds, Micheal C. *Race in Space: Representation of Ethnicity in Star Trek* (Lanham, Marland: Scarecrow Press, Inc.) 1999.

Porter, Jennifer E. and Darcee L. McLaren, editors. *Star Trek and Sacred Ground: Explorations of Star Trek, Religion and American Culture* (Albany, NY: State University of New York Press) 1999.

Porter, John. *The Tao of Star Wars* (Atlanta: GA, Humanics Publishing Group) 2003.

Premier: The Movie Magazine, "Special Collector's Issue," May 1999.

Publishers Weekly. "Lucasfilm Sues Little, Brown for Copyright Infringement" (Mar 15, 1999) p. 15.

Reddicliffe, Steven. "'Star Trek': 35th Anniversary Tribute," *TV Guide Magazine*, 2002.

Richards, Thomas. *The Meaning of 'Star Trek'* (New York: Doubleday) 1997.

Rosen, Steven J. *The Jedi in the Lotus: An Eastern Look at Star Wars* (to be published by Columbia University Press).

Rogers, Katherine. *L. Frank Baum: Creator of Oz* (New York: St. Martin's Press) 2002.

Ryan, Michael and Kellner Douglas. "George Lucas' Strategic Defense Initiatives," *Camera Politica: Politics and Ideology of Contemporary Hollywood Film* (Bloomington, IN: Indiana University Press) 1988, pp 228-236.

Sagan, Carl. *Contact* (New York: Pocket Books, 1985).

Sagan, Carl. *Cosmos* (New York: Random House, 2002).

Salvatore, R.A. *Star Wars: Episode II: Attack of the Clones* (New York: Del Rey Books, 2002).

Sansweet, Stephen J. *The Star Wars Encyclopedia* (New York: Ballantine Books, 1998).

Seay, Chris and Greg Garrett. *The Gospel Reloaded: Exploring Spirituality and Faith in the Matrix* (Colorado Springs, CO: Piñon Press) 2003.

Slavicsek Bill. *A Guide to the Star Wars Universe*, third edition (New York: Del Rey Books, 2000).

Snodgrass, Jon. *Follow Your Career Star: Career Quest Based on Inner Values* (New York: Kensington Publishing Corp., 1996).

Snodgrass, Jon. *On Becoming a Jedi Knight* (unpublised, 1997).

Snodgrass, Jon. 'Star Wars,' Terrorism and 'Attack of the Clones,' (filmthreat.com/features.asp?Id=526) August 2002.

Stone, Bryan P. *Faith and Film: Theological Themes at the Cinema* (St. Louis, MI: Chalice Press, 2000.

Thompson Anne. "The Big Bang," Interview with George Lucas, *Premiere: The Movie Magazine* May 1999) pp. 67-77.

Vidal, Gore. *Perpetual War for Perpetual Peace* (New York: Nation Books) 2002.

Vitas, Bob. Editor, *The Completely Unofficial Star Wars Encyclopedia*, Tenth Edition, May 2000 (moseisley.com).

Vogler, Christopher. *The Writer's Journey: Mytic Structure for Storytellers and Screen writers* (Studio City, CA: Michael Wiese Productions) 1992).

Voytilla, Stuart. *Myth and the Movies: Discovering the Mythic Structure of 50 Unforgettable Films* (Studio City, CA: Michael Wiese Productions) 1992.

Wachhorst, Wyn. *The Dream of Spaceflight* (New York: Basic Books, 2000).

Wapnick, Kenneth. *Love Does not Condemn* (Roscoe, NY: Foundation for "A Course in Miracles") 1989.

Wapnick, Kenneth. *A Talk Given on "A Course in Miracles"* (Roscoe, NY: Foundation for "A Course in Miracles") 1983.

Weber, Peter J. *The Incredible Internet Guide to Star Wars* (Tempe, AZ: Facts on Demand Press) 1999.

Weinraub, Bernard. "Luke Skywalker Goes Home" *Playboy*, July 1997.

Wilkinson, David. *The Power of the Force: The Spriritualiry of the 'Star Wars' Films*, (Oxford, England: Lion Publishing) 2000.

Yeffeth, Glenn ed. *Taking the Red Pill: Science, Philosophy and Religion in the Matrix* (Dallas, TX: Benbella Books) 2003.

Young, Jonathan. *'Star Wars' as Personal Mythology*, 1999 (folkstory.com).

Filmography

A New Hope (Twentieth Century Fox 1977) 23, 25, 29-33, 35, 60, 67, 79-83, 91, 103, 114, 128, 142, 151, 193
American Graffiti (Universal 1973) 42
Amores Perros (Altavista 2001) 19
Artificial Intelligence (Warner Studios 2001) 113
Attack of the Clones (Twentieth Century Fox 2002) 29, 31-32, 35, 141, 145, 160-165
Contact (Warner Studios 1997) 14
Cosmos: A Personal Voyage (Cosmos Studios 1980) 43
Empire Strikes Back The (Twentieth Century Fox 1980) 18, 24-25, 29-33, 35, 39, 57, 79, 91-95, 107-109, 124, 136-138, 142, 163, 189
Final Frontier The (Paramount 1989) 44
Forest Gump (Paramount Pictures 1994) 14, 42
Grand Illusion The (Criterion Collection 1938) 34
Jason and the Argonauts (Columbia Pictures 1963) 72
King Kong (RKO 1933) 94
K-PAX (Universal Studios 2001) 14, 204
Lion King (Disney Studios 1994) 93
Matrix The (Warner Studios 1999) 14, 17, 21, 30, 75, 84, 93, 107
Matrix The Reloaded (Warner Studios 2003) 15
Matrix The Revolutions (Warner Studios 2003) 16
Mulan (Disney Studios 1998) 154, 187
Nemesis (Paramount 2002) 45
Other Side of Midnight The (Twentieth Century Fox 1978) 30
Passion of the Christ The (Newmarket Film Group 2004) 77
Phantom Edit: Episode 1.01 (Unknown) 25, 50, 56, 59
Phantom Menace (Twentieth Century Fox 1999) 23, 24, 29-33, 35, 41, 50-59, 62, 137, 139, 148, 151-162, 164, 191
Powder (Hollywood Pictures 1995) 14
Return of the Jedi (Twentieth Century Fox 1983) 29-33, 35, 38, 62, 122-134, 144, 152, 154, 159, 194
Revenge of the Sith (Twentieth Century Fox 2005) 25-26, 32, 60, 137, 146, 157, 163
Seven Samurai The (Sojiro Motoki 1954) 35
Signs (Buena Vista 2002) 16, 204
Spider-Man (Columbia Pictures 2002) 32, 61, 72, 164
Spider-Man 2 (Columbia Pictures 2004) 164
Terminator 3 (Warner Brothers 2003) 74
Titanic (Paramount Pictures 1997) 29, 31-32
Wizard of Oz (MGM 1933) 55-56
Wrath of Khan (Paramount Pictures 1982) 130

Index

A

A Course in Miracles (ACIM) 14, 17, 51, 100-101, 113, 202, 204, 206
Adam and Eve 57
Allah 136
Allnutt, Frank 47
Amis, Robin 63
American Film Institute 30
Anger (attack, aggression, fury, hostility, rage) 17-18, 58, 60, 108, 57, 659, 106, 109, 111, 186, 193
Ankh (Anch) 74
Anti-Christ 59, 62, 136
Antiwar films 34
Arimathea, Joseph of 66
August, Pernilla 155

B

Backory, Anita 106
Barrett, Michèle and Duncan 43
Baum, L. Frank 55
Baxter, John 25
Beardsley, Aubrey 65-66
Bestian, Adolf 8
Blades, Kevin 24
Blavatsky, Helena Perovna 55
Bond, James 30
Bouzereau, Laurent 23, 155
Bridges, Jeff 14
Buddha (Buddhism) 14, 63, 71

C

Campbell, Joseph 8, 10, 40, 48, 55, 62
Cavelos, Jeane 39
Chaffey, Don 72
Chi 63
Chicago Sun Times 149
Chopra, Depak 55
Christianity 65, 75, 208
Christiansen, Hayden 149

Columbia Pictures 32, 72
Consciousness. See also Human Development 21-23, 200-206
Crosses 74-75
Cruz San Juan de la 75
Cruz, Sor Juana Inés de la 75

D

Dafoe, Willem 164
Dante Alighieri 49, 70
Darwin, Charles 202
Dawson, Roxann 44
Divine Comedy 70
DNA 25, 45, 51
Dualism 48, 191, 195, 205
Dunst, KIirsten 151

E

Ebert. Roger 149
Escher, M. C. 113
Egotism (selfish, self-centered, vanity, (narcissism) 121, 130, 136, 200, 203
Evil 25, 113, 116, 128-130, 136, 153-154, 161, 194-195
Excalibur 69-70

F

Fear 17, 82-83, 87, 104, 126, 152, 188, 195
Fighting 48, 62, 69, 109, 119, 126, 152, 159, 188, 192, 206
Film Threat 34
Fishburne, Laurence 16
Foster, Gloria 16
Ford, Harrison 41-42
Frank, Anne 128

G

Galileo 113
Gandhi, Mohandas 50, 161

Garden of Eden 53, 141
Garland, Judy 57-58
Gendai Geki 35
Gennep, Arnold van 8
Gibson, Mel 77, 204
God 16, 19, 22, 54, 57, 63-64, 70, 86, 90, 100, 105-106, 113-117, 133, 138, 140, 147, 186, 190-194, 203-210
Goethe, Johann Wolfgang von 75
Good and Bad (evil) 26, 48-53, 111, 164
Gospel of Thomas 93
Guilt 67, 90, 101, 105, 112, 120, 126, 138, 141, 145-146, 187-188, 191, 195, 199
Guinness, Sir Alec 69

H

Hamill, Mark 41-42, 50
Hanh, Thich Nhat 194
Hardy, Tom 45
Harryhausen, Ray 72
Harrison, Eric 25
Hate (hatred) 26, 119, 59, 152, 163, 207
Helen of Troy 72
Heisler, Bob 50
Hermes Trismegistus 22
Henderson, Mary 37, 50, 108
Hero
    Action (War) 13, 26, 37, 41, 81, 99, 140
    Wisdom (Peace) 13, 21-22, 27, 57-62, 86, 99, 186
Hinduism 63, 206
Holy Bible 53, 204
    Anakim 138
    Genesis 125
    Corinthians 186
    Isaiah 90
    Jonah and the Whale 79
    Last Supper 64
    Lucifer 66, 133
    Luke 63
    Matthew 4, 58, 126, 187, 201, 203
    Moses 58
    Noah 58
    Philippians 194, 207
    Psalms 111, 192
    Proverbs 112, 203
    Romans 101, 191
    Saint Paul 101, 134
    Saint Michael 66
Holy Sophia 53, 55, 74, 205
Homer 49, 69-70
Hugo, Victor 200
Human Development. See also Peace Knights.
    Adulthood 71-72, 156, 197-200
    Aging 71-72, 197-200
    Childhood 153-156, 197-200
    Death (Dying) 104, 126, 132, 198
    Maturity 21, 197-200
    Middle Adulthood 71-72, 198
    Midlife Crisis 71-72, 198
    Principles 13-18, 185-196
    Resistance 18, 21, 80, 83, 103
    Young Adulthood 71-72

I

Identity 23-28, 198
Islam 61, 63, 104, 134, 206, 208

J

Jason and the Argonauts 66, 72
Jeeva 63
Jenkins, Garry 38, 48, 50
Jesus Christ 58, 66, 92, 109, 205
Jidai Geki 35
Johnston, Joe 38
Jonah and the Whale 81
Jones, James Earl 25, 60
Judaism 49
Jung, C.G. 9, 27, 62

K

Kael, Pauline 40
Kelley, DeForrest 42
Kershner, Irvin 31, 139
King Arthur 57, 63, 67-71, 80, 202
King, Martin Luther 196

Koran (Quran) 106
Krishna 65
Kurasawa, Akira 37

L

Lady of the Lake 68, 74
Laurel and Hardy 56
Law of Faith (Rule of One) 35, 38, 52, 73
   86, 91, 105, 119, 135-136, 147, 186-187, 207
Lawrence, John 24
Leeper, Mark R. 30
Lieberman, Paul 50
Lien, Jennifer 44
Lloyd, Jake 150
Love
   Romantic 76, 81, 137-147
   Spiritual 136, 74-79
Los Angeles Times 26, 32, 51, 150
Lucas, George 9-10, 23, 29, 48, 35-36, 43-44, 50-52, 57, 64, 72, 118, 139
Lucas, Marcia 33
Lucifer 66, 135
Luckenbill, Laurence 47

M

MacArthur, Douglas 105, 125
Macguire, Tobey 164
Malebranche, Nicholas 117
Magdala (Magdalene) Mary 75
Malory, Sir Thomas 65
Marx, Karl 202
Marinaccio, Dave 40
Marquand, Richard 29
Matrix, The
   Characters
      Agent Smith 15, 204
      Morpheus 14
      Neo 14-16
      Oracle 14, 95
      Trinity 73, 75
Maturity 23, 199-202
McDiarmid, Ian 150

McGregor, Ewan 154
McVeigh, Timothy 26
Mentor(ing) 79-84, 91-101
Merlin the Magician 55, 61
Middle Ages 65
Mishnah 49
Mohs, Matthew C. 47, 54, 61, 121, 126
Molina, Alfred 164
Monism 111, 193, 205
Moyers, Bill 9, 36, 48
Muhammad 61
Mulgrew, Kate 42
Myths
   Garden of Eden 53, 59
   Jason and the Argonauts (Golden Fleece) 68, 72
   Helen of Troy 72-74
   Holy Grail 65-74
   Holy Sophia 55, 74-79
   King Arthur 67-72
Mysticism 62-64

N

Neeson, Liam 25, 155
Newton, Issac 14, 113, 201
New York Times 14
Nimoy, Leonard 40
Nord, Kevin M. 49, 65, 72, 138

O

Odysseus 70-72
Onassis, Aristotle 30
Oxford English Dictionary 37

P

Paramount Studios 39
Parables 26, 47
Prodigal Son 61
Park, Ray 154
Peace Knights
   Consciousness 21-23
   Gender and Sexuality 135-147
   Humor 18, 88, 96

Identity 23-28, 52, 62
Mind Power 21, 112-117, 194-196
Patience 21, 83, 95-99, 188-190
Phantom Enemy 21, 103-110, 190-194
Principles 13-18, 185-196
Resistance 83, 110-112
Training 18-21, 122-127
Willingness 21, 84–90, 185-188
Peace Phobia (Spirit Phobia) 11, 146
Perception (See projection)
Phantom Seduction 154
Playboy 48
Plato 14, 23, 107
Pollock, Dale 34, 37, 53, 137
Pontius Pilate 58
Portman, Natalie 151
Poseidon 71
Projection (perception) 13-15, 56, 84, 107, 110, 120, 135, 141, 191, 193, 201, 204
Prometheus 110
Publisher's Weekly 39

Q
Quran (Koran) 106

R
Racism and Sexism 27
Rational Faith. See also Law of Faith and Rule of One. 58-62, 88, 103
Reagan, Ronald 33, 36
Redemptive Violence
Reeves, Kenau 16
Renoir, Auguste 36
Renoir, Jean 36
Revenge (retaliation, vengeance, reprisal) 108, 126
Reverse Perspective 87-88, 93, 103, 113-119, 121, 123, 125, 144, 192
Rule of One 102
Rule of Two 101
Russ, Tim 46
Ryan, Jeri 45

S
Saint Michael 66
Saint Paul 132
Sagan, Carl 43
Satan (Devil) 57, 109, 121, 133
Science (Physics) 112-117
See-Thru-Pio 153
Shakespeare, William 21, 190
Shatner, William 40, 44
Snead, Elizabeth 47
Socrates 21, 92
Sophia Holy 53
Spanish 50, 79, 111, 113, 96
Spiner, Brent 45
Spritual Consciousness. See Human Development
Spirit Phobia (Peace Phobia) 11, 146
Spoilers 32, 137, 157, 163
Star Trek
    Characters
        B4 45
        Bones 44
        B'Elanna Torres 44
        Captain James T. Kirk 40
        Captain Jean Luc Picard 45
        Captain Kathryn Janeway 44
        Data 45
        Doctor McCoy 40
        Kes 44
        Mister Spock 40, 44
        Seven of Nine 43-44
        Shinzon 45
        Sybok 44-45
        Tuvok 44
Star Trek Enterprise 44
Star Trek: Next Generation The 45
Star Trek: Original Series The (TOS) 37-39, 50
Star Trek Voyager 42-44
Star Wars
    Conspiracy 160-165
    Characters
        Anakin Skywalker 26, 31, 52, 62, 97, 109, 111, 132-133, 150-151, 153-160, 162, 199

Artoo Detoo 57, 73, 80-83, 97, 107, 112, 123 153
Binks, Jar Jar 25, 56
Darth Sidious 150
Darth Maul 31, 33, 71, 106, 150, 152
Darth Vader 48, 57, 59-60, 62, 80, 92, 104-105, 120-122, 127-134, 107, 110, 138, 150, 190, 194-199
Emperor Palpatine 48, 58, 107-108, 127-129, 130-131, 162-163
Han Solo 41-42, 63, 79, 93, 121-1264 137, 141-147
Jar Jar Binks 56, 160
Leia Skywalker 38, 57-60, 73-74, 79, 81, 120, 122, 125, 130, 135, 141-147,151
Luke Skywalker 18, 41, 47, 57-62, 72, 79-83, 91-98, 101, 103-108, 112, 114-115, 119-120, 127-134, 151, 154, 190, 193, 195-197
Obi-Wan Kenobi 33, 47, 52, 57, 59, 61-62, 69, 80, 97, 99-101, 107, 111
Padmé Amidala Skywalker 60, 125-126, 133, 149-151, 152, 160
Qui-Gon Jinn 24, 33, 151-160
See-Threepio 57, 95, 153-154, 161
Shmi Skywalker 137, 153-156
Sith The 24, 26, 100
Uncle Owen 61, 121, 125
Yaddle 137
Yoda 18, 22, 33, 47, 55, 57, 74, 82, 91-99, 103, 114, 119-120, 124-127, 133, 137-139, 156-165, 190
Force The 16, 38, 47, 57, 93, 103, 194, 198, 201
History 29-37
Jedi Knights 16, 20, 33, 48, 52-53, 57, 64, 82, 92, 103, 109
Jedi Knights Female 135-137, 156
Midi-chlorian 23-25, 155-156
Sith 26, 100, 149-152, 160-165, 191
Sexuality 135-147, 154-155
Theology 37-39, 47-64
Stewart, Patrick 45

T

Tai Chi Chuan 63
Taoism 62, 90
Test
  Blood 155-157
  Character 19, 82, 85, 106, 156-161

Time Magazine 33, 36, 48, 160
Tolstoy, Leo 51
Torah 49
Twentieth Century Fox Studios 30, 33, 69
Twins 53, 73
Tzu, Lao 90

V

Violence 19, 105, 191, 193, 202
Vitas, Robert 189

W

War and Peace 51
Ward, James 33
Washington Post 36
Wilkinson, David 47
Williams, Billie Dee 25
Williams, John 30

Y

Young, Jonathan 7-10, 25, 50, 62-63

Z

Zeus 70, 72

Glossary

ACIM: *A COURSE IN MIRACLES*
ACRONYM: WORD FORMED FROM THE INITIAL LETTERS OF A NAME.
ADEPT: EXPERT
AMULET: TANGIBLE REMINDER OF FAITH USUALLY WORN AND OFTEN INSCRIBED.
ANAGRAM: WORD GAME REARRAGNING LETTERS TO FIND A HIDDEN MESSAGE.
ANDERSON: SON OF MAN
ANDROGENY: BISEXUAL APPEARANCE AND PERSONALITY NOT DIVIDED BY SEX ROLE SOCIALIZATION.
ANDROID: COMPUTERIZED ROBOT DESIGNED IN HUMAN FORM.
ARCHETYPE: BASIC MODEL, IDEAL TYPE, TEMPLATE.
AVANT-GARDE: FUTURISTIC.
AUTOMATONS: HUMANS WHO ACT LIKE MACHINES.
CANON: WRITINGS CONSIDERED AUTHENTIC BY EXPERTS OR AUTHORITIES.
CONSCIOUSNESS: BEING AWARE OF A COLLECTIVELY SHARED MENTAL STATE OF ONENESS.
COUP D'ÉTAT: OVERTHROW OF THE STATE BY A SMALL GROUP.
COUP DE GRACE: DEATH BLOW OF MERCY TO END SUFFERING.
DEBORGED: RESCUED FROM THE BORG RACE WHO CONVERT SPECIES INTO AUTOMATONS.
EPONYMOUS: THE PERSON FOR WHOM SOMETING IS NAMED.
ESOTERIC: KNOWN ONLY TO INSIDERS.
GENOME: UNIT OF GENETIC INHERITANCE.
GNOME: AGELESS ELF IN FOLKLORE.
HERMES TRISMEGISTUS: (THREE TIMES GREAT) ANCIENT LEGENDARY TEACHER IN EGYPT SAID TO BE AN EARLIER INCARNATION OF JESUS.
INTRAPSYCHIC: WITHIN THE MIND.
MISCEGENATION: SEXUAL INTERCOURSE OR MARRIAGE BETWEEN RACES.
METAPHOR: ABSTRACT IDEA PUT IN STORY FORM.
METAPHYSICS: META = "ABOVE" PHYSICS OR STUDY OF ABSTRACT PRINCIPLES GOVERNING LIFE.
NOVICE: BEGINNER.
OXYMORON: CONCEPT WITH CONTRADICTORY TERMS.
PADAWAN: APPRENTICE
PALIMPSEST: REUSED STONE TABLET.
PRESCIENCE: FOREKNOWLEDGE
PROMETHEUS: A TITAN IN GREEK MYTHOLOGY WHO RULED THE EARTH UNTIL DEFEATED BY THE GODS OF OLYMPUS. HE STOLE FIRE AND THE ARTS FROM HEAVEN TO GIVE HUMANITY AND WAS PUNISHED BY ZEUS CHAINED TO A MOUNTAINSIDE WHERE HE WAS ATTACKED BY A VULTURE FOR ETERNITY.
PSYCHOKINESIS: THE ABILITY TO MOVE PHYSICAL OBJECTS WITH THE MIND.
REALPOLITIK: POLITICS BASED ON MIGHT RATHER THAN ETHICS.
REDEMTIVE VIOLENCE: SAVED BY USING VIOLENT MEANS.
SPOILER: INFORMATION DIVULGED BY VIEWERS OR REVIEWERS REVEALING THE PLOT OR ENDING OF A FILM.
THEOSOPHY: ANCIENT SPIRITUALITY BASED ON MYSTICAL INSIGHT AND METAPHYSICAL MOVEMENT IN THE U. S. IN THE LATE 19TH CENTURY LEAD BY HELENA PEROVNA BLAVATSKY.
TORAH: SACRED SCRIPTURE OF JUDIASM AND FIRST FIVE BOOKS OF THE CHRISTIAN BIBLE.
TROLL: FIGURE IN FOLKLORE: DWARF, ELF, GNOME, GENIE, HOBGOBLIN, IMP, OGRE, SPRITE.

Contributors

Paulo Dionisio
I was born in the Philippines in 1979 and raised there as a child. I came to the United States for a few years and returned to the Philippines when I was sixteen. After graduation from high school I returned again to the United States. I am finishing my degree at California State University, Los Angeles, in computer science though I still long to be a musician.

Lucho Calvo-Guerrero
I was born and raised in the City of Los Angeles twenty-four years ago. I graduated from California State University, Los Angeles with a major in political science. I am working as a teacher's assistant. I plan to teach high school government and history. As a hobby I like building and repairing computers. I am trying to be at peace, put everything behind me and start fresh.

Qiao (Jo) Kang
I am a nineteen-year old Chinese female born in Beijing. I moved to the United States in 1996 and obtained my high school diploma from Arcadia High School. I am a student at California State University, Los Angeles. My culture has an impact on me but I have focused on learning English and my passion is reading fiction. I like creative writing and I am expanding my fondness for this soul seeking activity.

Mui Lam
My family immigrated to the Unites States when I was five years old from Hong Kong where I was born in 1978. I grew up in metropolitan Los Angeles, and like the city, I find myself very busy. I am a graduate of California State University with a degree in computer information systems and accounting. I work as a legal secretary and live at home with my parents, three brothers and sister.

Mariano E. Meléndez
I currently live with my Pit Bull-Labrador in Silver Lake, California. I continue my education at California State University, Los Angeles while working at various nameless jobs. My free time is spent riding waves or enjoying the evening breezes on the trails of Elysian Park. I am also trying to pursue a relatively stress-free existence.

Jonathan Young

I am a psychologist, storyteller and author. I was assistant to mythologist Joseph Campbell and Founding Curator (1990-1995) of the Joseph Campbell Archives and Library at the Pacifica Graduate Institute, Santa Barbara, CA and chaired the Mythological Studies Department. I am now Director of the Center for Story and Symbol and teach mythic stories using depth psychology (folkstory.com). I edit *SAGA: Best New Writings on Mythology* (White Cloud Press). I live with my cats in an old house in Santa Barbara.

Jon Snodgrass

I was born in Colón, Republic of Panamá and hold U. S. and Panamanian citizenship. I was educated in U.S. government schools in the former Panama Canal Zone. I obtained B.A. and M.A. degrees from the University of Maryland and a Ph.D. from the University of Pennsylvania (1972). Professor of Sociology, California State University, Los Angeles for more than thirty years teaching child and adult development, and small group dynamics.

I hold a second Ph.D. in child psychoanalytic psychotherapy from the Reiss-Davis Child Study Center in West Los Angeles (1985). I am licensed as a psychotherapist in private practice in South Pasadena, California. Previously I authored three books: *Follow Your Career Star: Career Quest Based on Inner Values* (Kensington, 1996); *The Jack-Roller at Seventy: A Follow-Up of 'A Delinquent Boy's Own Story'* (Lexington, 1982); and *For Men Against Sexism: A Book of Readings* (Times Change Press, 1977).

>**Jon Snodgrass, Ph.D.**
>Department of Sociology
>California State University
>Los Angeles, CA 90032
>(323) 343-2215
>jsnodgr@calstatela.edu

Readers!
Visit us online at www.innercirclepublishing.com and browse our new releases. Take advantage of ordering direct and receive a 25% discount off all titles.

Authors!
Do you have a book to publish?
Would you like to make it available world-wide?
Available online through all bookstores?

Contact us:
Revolution Press
406 Bissell Street
Laurens, Iowa 50554
www.rev-press.com

Booksellers!
Are you interested in offering a new genre of books?
Contact us about wholesale offers.

InnerCircle Publishing

Metaphysical. Poetry. Spiritual. Aware. Philosophical. Insightful. Uplifting. Life Changing. Mind-altering. Informative. Intangible. Honest. Unity. Conductive to elements that align the body, soul, and mind to listen to the conscience.

Catalog of Original Titles

ISBN	Title
0-9720080-9-8	the sometimes girl by Lisa Zaran
0-9720080-2-0	Return To Innocence by Dr. Steven Hairfield
0-9723191-4-X	Poetry to Touch the Heart and Soul by Marla Wienandt
0-9723191-2-3	Because Why? The Journey Once Asked! by Kirstie Silk
0-9723191-3-1	Falling Awake by Royal Atman
0-9723191-1-5	The Divine Plan by Vicki Fletcher
0-9723191-9-0	Handwriting on the Wall - ICP Original Anthology
0-9723191-8-2	Stress Fractures by Andew Lewis
0-9723191-6-6	Life Rhymes by Rene Ferrell
0-9723191-7-4	One Hundred Keys to the Kingdom by Prince Camp, Jr.
0-9723191-0-7	the voice by Rick LaFerla
0-9723191-5-8	A Day in the Mind by Chad Lilly
0-9720080-3-9	Interview With An American Monk by Dr. Steven Hairfield
0-9755214-7-0	Peace Knights of the Soul by Dr. Jon Snodgrass
0-9755214-0-3	On the Edge of Deceny by Rick LaFerla
0-9755214-6-2	uncommon sense by Chad Lilly
0-9755214-8-9	Warrior-Poet of the Fifth Sun by Luis A. López
0-9755214-1-1	Petals of a Flower by Patricia McHenry
0-9755214-2-X	Poetry-Prose-Stories by J.L. Montgomery
0-9755214-9-7	Touched by Spirit by Marla Wienandt

Are You Aware?
www.innercirclepublishing.com